It's Never Too Late to Be Happy

Reparenting Yourself for Happiness

It's Never Too Late to Be Happy

Reparenting Yourself for Happiness

BY
MURIEL JAMES

Fresno, California

Quill Driver Books
An imprint of Linden Publishing
2006 S. Mary Street
Fresno, California 93721
(559) 233-6633
800-345-4447

QuillDriverBooks.com

Printed in the United States of America

Quill Driver Books books may be purchased in quantity at special prices for educational, fund-raising, business, or promotional use.
Please contact:

Special Markets
Quill Driver Books
2006 S. Mary Street
Fresno, California 93721
800-345-4447

Quill Driver Books
Project Cadre:
Doris Hall • Dave Marion • Stephen Blake Mettee • Brigitte Phillips • Linda Kay Weber

To order a copy of this book, please call 1-800-345-4447.

ISBN 1-844956-26-2

Library of Congress Cataloging-in-Publication Data

James, Muriel.

It's never too late to be happy : reparenting yourself for happiness / by Muriel James. -- New, rev. 3rd ed.

p. cm.

Includes bibliographical references and index.

ISBN 1-884956-26-2

1. Transactional analysis. 2. Happiness. I. Title.

RC489.T7 J355 2001

158.1--dc21

2001031830

Praise for

It's Never Too Late to Be Happy!

"A wonderfully encouraging book for turning our lives around."
—*Reiko Homma True, Ph. D., Assistant Professor*
University of California, San Francisco, Department
of Psychiatry

"*It's Never Too Late to Be Happy!* helps in understanding why people react the way they do. It provides the language, knowledge base, and foundation to use to gain greater self-understanding, acceptance of the impact of the past, and separation of the past from the present in order to create the desired changes."
—*W. Edward Davis, M.D., M.B.A., M.M.M.,*
Section Head, Allergy and Immunology, Ochsner
Clinic Foundation, New Orleans, Louisiana

". . . a wonderful guide to understand the steps to personal power."
—*Brenda Mabry, Executive Coach*

"The perfect program for developing a synergy among all aspects of our lives: loving, thinking, working, playing."
—*Dr. Camille Minichino, Author and Physicist*

"*It's Never Too Late to Be Happy!* provides a proven and practical path to recover happiness. Through applying the process of self-reparenting, readers will be able to restore their personal security and vitality."
—*Rev. Denton L. Roberts, Marriage, Family, Child*
Therapist

Books Authored and Coauthored by Muriel James

Psychology and Personal Growth:
Born to Win: Transactional Analysis With Gestalt Experiments (1971, new edition 1996)
A New Self: Self Therapy with Transactional Analysis (1977)
Techniques in Transactional Analysis for Psychotherapists and Counselors (1977)
Breaking Free: Self Re-Parenting for a New Self (1981)
It's Never Too Late to Be Happy: Self-Reparenting with Transactional Analysis (1985, new edition, 2002*)*
Perspectives in Transactional Analysis (1998)

Management Training:
Winning With People (1973)
The OK Boss (1973)
Winning Ways in Health Care (1981)
The Better Boss in Multicultural Organizations (1991)

Families and Friends:
Marriage Is For Loving (1979)
What Do You Do With Them Now That You've Got Them? (1974)
The People Book: Transactional Analysis For Young Students (1973)
The Heart of Friendship (1976)

Spiritual Dimensions:
Born to Love: Transactional Analysis and the Church (1973)
The Power at the Bottom of the Well (1974)
Passion for Life: Psychology and the Human Spirit (1991)

History:
Hearts on Fire: Romance and Achievement In The Lives Of Great Women (1991)
Religious Liberty On Trial (1997)

....

Muriel James books have been translated into 22 languages.

Contents

1

An Action Plan for Happiness

Do you ever ask yourself questions about how to feel happier or how to feel happy more often?

Do you ever feel depressed because you can't seem to hold on to the happiness you felt in the past?

Do you ever wonder about your chances of being really happy in the future?

If you answered yes to any of the above, this book is for you. It is an action plan to increase your chances for happiness, even if you thought you'd given up on being happy. Lots of things interfere with a person's being happy—a bad marriage, an unpleasant job, difficult relationships, not enough money, a sad experience, being treated unfairly. But even if life hasn't always seemed fair to you, you do have another chance at happiness, and only you can make it happen. *It's never too late to be happy!*

A Look Ahead

In a career exploration workshop where people were discussing possible job changes, one woman said, "It doesn't matter too much what kind of work I will do because I am going to make a career out of being happy."

In this first chapter, we will examine the definition of happiness and consider happiness as a "choice" rather than as a "right." We will discuss the origins of personality and explore a current psychological theory for understanding personality. Finally, we will preview the remaining chapters in this book that make up the "action plan" for attaining true happiness. As you work your way through the succeeding chapters and complete the exercises that accompany each chapter, you may feel as if you have discovered a gold mine within yourself, or the capacity to find one.

In life, many things seem to occur by chance. Other things occur by design. This book gives you a design for happiness. The design is an action plan that really can work—if you want it to work and are willing to try it out.

Defining the Word

In order to prepare yourself for this action plan, think for a moment. If you were writing a dictionary, how would you define happiness? How do you feel, talk, and act when you are happy? At what times in your life did you deeply experience this wonderful feeling?

Everyone hopes for happiness, but for many, it seems to be beyond reach. It doesn't have to be that way. If you were to wake up in the morning and think, "I'm going to be happy today," what would that mean to you? Would it mean you would experience happiness during the routine of the day? Would it mean you would expect happiness only if you were to achieve or acquire something? Is it possible that both can be true? Is happiness for you a tangible or an intangible? Can happiness be created? Can it be sought after? Or, is happiness just "something that comes to a person"?

Happiness sometimes comes as a surprise—for example, when you receive an unexpected gift such as a warm sweater in your favorite color in the midst of a winter freeze. Happiness may also come with less surprise but equal pleasure if you perform and are applauded for playing a piano concerto that you practised with great diligence.

> "Cherish all your happy moments; they make a fine cushion for old age."
> —Christopher Morley

Moments of elation can also be experienced when you have a creative idea, a visit from a dear friend, or a paycheck that enables you to pay all your bills. When your body functions well, when the weather is the kind you like, when your dog welcomes you eagerly or your cat purrs in your lap, when the flowers you planted bloom, when the meal you prepared turns out just right, and when the people you are with are interesting and enjoyable. We've all known similar moments and want more of them. How can we become more aware of the innumerable possibilities for happiness? How can we become aware of the many ways we can turn possibilities into realities?

Although happiness is usually associated with *feeling* good, an understanding of how we interpret happiness for ourselves is useful. Some people only achieve happiness when they finish a task, while others are happy with that which precedes the finish. For example, when making love, some people are happiest at the climax, while others are happier during the process that leads up to it. As another example, in competitive sports happiness is more likely to be felt at the moment of winning, while in noncompetitive sports, like hiking or river rafting, happiness is more likely to lie in the process; arriving at the chosen destination is important, yet it seldom tops the excitement of getting there.

How you define happiness is critical, both to create satisfaction in your life and for you to gain the benefits of this book. If you have a clear definition of happiness, one that is grounded in reality, and a clear idea of what you believe could make you happy in life, then, and only then, can you pursue happiness. If you don't know what happiness is, you won't be likely to recognize it when you find it.

In this book, we will look at the process of pursuing happiness as well as achieving hoped-for goals. You will find that achieving happiness will include reparenting yourself (more about that shortly), training yourself, encouraging yourself, and building your skills and self-esteem. You will learn that true happiness isn't always dependent on specific events in your life. True happiness grows out of adjusting your outlook—so that the good things in your life take precedence over the bad.

Life, Liberty, and the Pursuit of Happiness

Most people would agree that being guaranteed life, liberty, and the pursuit of happiness has enormous value.

However, no one is guaranteed happiness; happiness

cannot be a state-given right. What is guaranteed in life is only the right to pursue happiness. That right to pursue happiness involves a choice. You, yourself, and only yourself, can make the choice to pursue happiness and to be or to become happy.

And, to pursue happiness often requires a basic redecision about the *right* to be happy. Children, consciously or subconsciously, make decisions about whether they are entitled to love and happiness. Many childhood decisions are not realistic nor conducive to growth. Often these decisions change in response to evolving situations or are deliberately redecided.

The effects of childhood are with us long after we become adults but, as we'll see, we have the ability to reevaluate them and take control of our thoughts and actions. To move from discontentment to happiness, we need to convince ourselves that happiness comes in different forms and we are at liberty to find it in different situations.

Experiencing happiness and actively pursuing happiness give added dimensions to life. This book is about how to liberate yourself from some of the effects of negative experiences. Then you can live life more fully with greater chances of success in finding the happiness you've always wanted.

In the Beginning

You were born as the result of an egg and a sperm coming together. You had no choice in the matter. Also, you had no choice as to who your parents were, their race, their ethnic origin, their financial situation, or even the location of their home. Finally, you had no control or choice over the education, the stability, the personalities, or the parenting skills possessed by your parents. You may or may not have been wanted, may or may not have been physically and emotionally healthy, your parents may or may not have had adequate resources to provide adequate care for you. Whatever the situation, you probably wished from time to time that your parents had given you something more.

That "something more" could have been more tenderness, more sympathy for your hurts, more protection from ridicule, more encouragement for your academic achievements, more appreciation for you as a person, or more freedom to be you.

You may wish that your parents had shown you how to do more things, or that they had listened to your ideas and accepted your feelings when you expressed them. Whatever your age now, you may still feel angry if your parents were preoccupied with their own interests and didn't treat you as if you were important. You may still feel deeply sad if your parents died or deserted you. You may have wondered from time to time what you would be like now if your parents had been different.

Perhaps your parents constantly urged you to be on time, to hurry. "Don't be late!" can be a useful message if children are dawdling in the morning before school. But too much rushing gives a child another message: "Don't take time to enjoy!" Children (and adults) occasionally need the kind of enjoyment that comes from watching a flower open to the sun, even when there are tasks to be accomplished.

When they are constantly pressured, children may grow

to believe that there is no time to enjoy the beautiful moments of living: when happiness flashes with its myriad of colors across the mind's horizon, when the "music of the spheres" is heard as a beautiful symphony of sound, when one's body moves in harmony with the dance of life. The child who hurries to avoid being "too late" may grow up to be an adult who feels he or she is always too late.

The point is that many children receive messages that are debilitating. The input they receive is flawed, antidevelopmental, and negative. This input, unfortunately, becomes imprinted, or programmed, on their being and becomes a huge negative personality influence.

But it is not too late. It is not too late to catch happiness as it flies, and to enjoy the process of doing so.

Most people have experienced the sense of being outside of time. They may be surprised when they look at the clock and note that what felt like seconds was measured in hours, or what seemed like hours was measured in minutes. Regardless of the unhappiness in your past, you can live now, feeling alive and expectant as you take time, or move outside of time, to discover it's never too late to be happy.

This book will show you that whatever you thought and felt about your parents then, whatever you think and feel about them now, you can revise your perspectives. You can also revise your present and future life by building something new into your personality. This new something in your personality will serve as a new "positive" parent, or as an encouraging coach or mentor who will assist you in your search for happiness.

Personality Perspectives

There is no firm agreement on the meaning of *personality*. As the word comes from the Latin *persona*, which means "mask," some theorists claim personality is what a person shows to the world while hiding other parts of the self. Other theorists see personality as a complex set of responses that are observable. "You are what you do" is their orientation. They de-emphasize the hidden aspects of personality.

Still other theorists view personality from a "self theory" and focus on the internal mechanism that controls behavior. Some believe in "trait theory." Traits are inherited or acquired and tend to be persistent. They are part of the neuropsychic system that determines how we perceive our environment and the events and relationships in our lives.

> "I always prefer to believe the best in everybody—it saves so much trouble."
> —Rudyard Kipling

Whatever orientation is given to the word *personality*, it is generally agreed that personality can be described in terms of *consistent behavior patterns*. However, there is no general agreement on the *origins* of those consistent behavior patterns. The disagreement, sometimes called the "nature versus nurture" or "genes versus environment" controversy, is generations old and continues to be debated.

The nature side of this controversy can be recognized in a statement such as "He inherited his temper from his father." This indicates a belief in the "nature," or genetic, origin of certain consistent behavior patterns—one inherits one's personality and can do little, if anything, to alter that personality throughout life. Someone taking the opposite point of view, the "nurture" or environmental position, could make the statement "What can you expect of a person from that background!" This indicates a belief that family patterns, attitudes, values, and actions—indeed, the total culture and environment in which one is raised—is what determines personality.

Most theorists today believe both views are true and each affects the makeup of our personality. The effects of inherited genes on personality are real. So, too, are the effects of many cultural determinants. Yet, each theorist is likely to stress one position more than the other.

This author's orientation is one that recognizes the impact of inherited traits, yet focuses more directly on the many cultural determinants, including the backgrounds of our parents, the development of our unique family systems, and the effects of teachers, peers, and other significant persons who sometimes function as our substitute parents or as additional parent-types.

A Theory for Understanding Personality

Many psychological systems do not have a personality theory. Personality is assumed, but the structure of it—the whys of its development and the hows of changing its structure—are widely ignored.

Transactional analysis (often abbreviated as TA) has a specific personality theory first developed by psychiatrist Eric Berne, M.D. in the late 1950s. It was expanded by others, including this writer. Using the concepts of transactional analysis, you can discover what went wrong in your childhood, how the powerful influences of your parents, both real and surrogates (teachers, coaches, etc.), molded and shaped your personality. The foundation of the transactional analysis theory is that there are three major parts to everyone's personality. These are called the Parent ego state, the Adult ego state and the Child ego state. (When capitalized in this book, these words—Parent, Adult, and Child—will refer to personality ego states. When not capitalized, they will refer to people—your actual parents and other adults who sometimes served as parent-figures, and you, yourself as a child.)

People respond to other people, to the events in their lives, to their environment, and to themselves using one of their three ego states. The Parent ego state reacts and interacts in terms of value expression and attitude. These values and attitudes were largely determined by the values and attitudes of your parents during your childhood. The Child ego state reacts and interacts in terms of emotions, much like a child would. These emotions were shaped during your childhood in *response* to the values and attitudes of your parents. The Adult ego state, which often acts as a referee between the Parent ego state and the Child ego state, reacts and interacts rationally and analytically. This rationality and analytical ability are shaped as a child grows up and learns the day-to-day survival skills for living in the real world.

The transactional analysis diagram of personality is represented by three stacked circles: the Parent at the top, the Child at the bottom, and the Adult between the two. Psychological energy often moves between ego states depending on the situation. For example, each ego state may have a different belief system about the value of freedom and happiness, and the clear-thinking Adult may need to referee between the Parent and the Child to decide what is practical and possible.

When people are in the Parent ego state, they are likely to have opinions similar to those their parent figures once had and to act in similar ways if they have incorporated parent figures into their own personalities, often without awareness of having done so. For example, as were their parents, they may be critical of people who do not agree with them, or nurturing toward people who need help, or indifferent to those who want to be listened to.

When people are in the Child ego state, they feel and act as they did when they were young—with curiosity and enthusiasm, sadness and withdrawal, anger and rebellion, compliance and hopelessness, just as they tended to act during their childhood. The younger children are, the freer they are to act spontaneously and express their feelings openly. But as they are growing up, they often give up the freedom to express feelings naturally and struggle to modify qualities that might be disapproved of by parent figures.

When people are in the Adult ego state, they are processing material in the here and now. They observe, compute, analyze, and make decisions on the basis of facts, not fancy. Being grown up is not the same as being in the Adult ego state. Many grown-ups sometimes act like children or parental dictators in inappropriate ways.

A refereeing Adult may be necessary when the Parent ego state, like a videotape, is turned on knowingly or unknowingly. When it is on, old slogans, injunctions, permissions, and directions are replayed. But like old computer software, internal messages may need upgrading.

When Parent messages are heard internally, the inner Child may comply, rebel, procrastinate, or try to ignore them. If that same person uses old Parent tapes toward others, the others may also respond by complying, rebelling, or ignoring the messages.

Much of the dialogue that goes on inside people's heads is about expectations between the Parent and Child. At one time in everyone's personal history, the parent figures were real people who could be seen, heard, and touched. Then the parents became incorporated into the Parent ego state.

So, too, the Child was once a real little boy or girl who became covered by the body of a grown-up. Though covered and hidden, the Child remains active, especially when hearing internal parent messages (as she or he once heard), or external parent messages. External parent messages often come from others on the job or in the home, and a person's responses to them are often the same as they were in childhood to similar messages from their real parents.

Thus, each of the ego states is, in effect, a system of communication, with its own language and function; the Parent's is a language of values and attitudes, the Adult's is a language of logic and rationality, and the Child's is a language of emotions. Effective functioning in the world depends on the availability of all three ego states. Each ego state has an appropriate time and place to express itself in reaction to and interaction with our environments, our relationships, and the events we experience. Often, however, inappropriate or self-defeating emotional responses occur because we have been over-programmed by aversive early-life events to respond from one ego state when another would be far more appropriate. The inability to recognize the inappropriate ego state and make the transition to the more effective ego state often leads to profound unhappiness in life.

There is hope, however. In order to repair this imbalance and open a new doorway to happiness, people can actually reprogram their Parent ego state; through self-examination and a new understanding of the elements of their personality which were products of their parents' values and attitudes, they can begin the process of self-reparenting.

> *"Imagination is more important than knowledge."*
> —*Albert Einstein*

When the Parent part of the personality is restructured, a person often experiences a sense of liberation and the freedom to be happy.

Imagining a New Life

Relax for just a moment. Imagine how life would be if you were freed from some negative self-images and consequently had more self-esteem. Imagine having high energy to put into things that are important to you and that could increase your happiness. Imagine what the world could be like if people were committed to helping each other become liberated and committed to encouraging each other to be happy.

All people have the capacity to imagine. We are born with it. Because of this, we can visualize an environment where we are free to grow and change. Visualization has been proven to be a potent tool in physical and emotional change. Negative visualization often leads to negative results. Visualizing oneself to be healthy and happy motivates a person to pursue health and happiness.

This book will help you make real what you have imagined. It is an action plan. As you free yourself from some of the negative self-images you carry from the past and create a new, supportive, encouraging Parent, who will guide you lovingly through the challenges of life, you will experience happiness more often and for longer periods of time than you thought possible. At the core of your being, you will know the increasing strength that comes when you direct your energies to making your hope of happiness a reality.

Complying, Rebelling, and Withdrawing Responses

Many people feel unhappy or inadequate because as children they did not receive enough positive affirmations, and they do not now feel entitled to give similar positive affirmations to themselves. They put a low value on their own rights to life and liberty and happiness. They need a new inner Parent to encourage them, one that will function more like a good mentor or coach instead a controlling, overprotective, or indifferent parent.

Parenting is what actual parents, stepparents, foster parents or grandparents do and say to children as they are growing up. Generally, they take care of their children, teach them, guide them, and even play with them. Some do it well, others fail dismally or are just so-so—partly competent and partly incompetent at the task.

Some parents, even after their children become adults, continue to treat them as though they were still very young by directly or indirectly telling them what to do and how to do it. These parents don't want to give up their advice-giving roles and may try to restrict their grown children in many ways.

In response to this kind of controlling parent, some children remain obedient and relinquish their chance to experience freedom and happiness. Feeling inadequate to take charge of their own lives, they tend to comply with inappropriate or unnecessary controls and restrictions. Others, instead of complying, choose to rebel directly or they procrastinate or, feeling hopeless, try to avoid being around people who use controlling styles.

Since the beginning of time, persons have acted as substitute parents to others—with or without awareness of it. Women have done this more frequently than men, yet men have also assumed parenting functions. Both fiction and nonfiction and ancient and contemporary history are full of examples of grandparents, aunts, uncles, older siblings, even friends, who acted as substitute parents. Even an institution may perform this role and shape the development of a child in positive or negative ways.

The most common substitute parents are teachers, and healthy children tend to seek out teachers who support their independence and growth and avoid those who interfere with it. A teacher who repeatedly says "You're very intelligent" may effectively reparent a child who originally was programmed with "You're stupid."

In many cases, these teachers are so influential that they are incorporated into the personalities of their charges without awareness. If a teacher's values are perceived as overly critical or too much like a parent back home, children often lose their natural incentive to learn. If teachers' values are positive and encouraging, there are likely to be positive results. Substitute parenting by teachers, psychotherapists, or others does not necessarily lead to a sense of independence and feelings of happiness. But, in the process of *self-reparenting,* these positive values are more likely to occur.

The Essence of Self-reparenting

Self-reparenting is a new theory and procedure for changing the Parent ego state. It has been tested and proven by standardized psychological tests to be effective. It is an action plan that you can use to reprogram yourself.

We have all been partially programmed, even before birth. Now, in the age of technology and the expanding use of computers, we recognize that with specific software we can interact with the computer's hardware to perform specific tasks. For example, with a word-processing program we can change the text of what we put down on paper. Remnants of the old text may be saved, but the new text will be different according to the choices we make.

A similar process goes on in self-reparenting. The word "self" is important because it indicates that you *will decide for yourself* what you need to delete, change, or add to the Parent ego state part of your personality so you feel encouraged and able to pursue new happiness.

Based on your own decision to update your old inner Parent, the program in this book uses specific procedures so that you can decrease the power past parent figures have over you. You can create and add additional parent figures, such as a coach who can train your inner Child how to win as an individual in the pursuit of happiness, or win as part of a team. Or, you can create and add a mentor who may be more like a teacher to you as an individual, but who can also instruct you on how to win in your search.

In self-reparenting, you may or may not choose to discard specific positive or negative remnants of your historical parent figures that are now in the Parent part of your personality.

Instead, you will add an extra new parent figure that you create for yourself and who will have positive qualities your own parents might not have had, or might have had but did not express to you. The positive qualities of this new part of your personality will be the ones you decide you want to develop in order to enhance your life in ways that lead to happiness.

Some characteristics in your Parent ego state are okay. Other characteristics may not be. With self-reparenting, you will be able to turn off your internal, outdated programs that contain negative qualities that might interfere with your continuing growth and happiness. This will add to your strengths. You will learn how to be more effective in taking charge of your life and changing what you decide you want to change.

The Importance of Teachers, Mentors, and Coaches

Many people who are parents see their tasks as unique, and they surely are. In addition to providing food, clothing, and shelter, they teach, mentor, and coach their children.

As most parents discover, this is not always easy, as these roles are often blended. Delineating the differences in roles is not simple. Generally speaking, teachers are most often thought of as those who work in classrooms and instruct, guide, and sometimes discipline groups of students. Mentors also give instruction and guidance, but usually to individual students in selected subjects or for a particular purpose.

Coaches are most common in athletics training others to succeed in several sports or in a particular sport. Their training focuses on improving individual skills and, in some sports, improving teamwork.

The word "coaching" has recently become popular in nonathletic fields. Many parents and psychotherapists are seeing the value of using a coaching approach and paying special attention to how physical health relates to performance—individually and as part of a team.

Because parents, including stepparents, grandparents, adoptive, and foster parents, are usually encountered first in children's lives, they have strong influence on later development. Other authority figures, such as teachers, mentors, or coaches are seldom experienced before school years. By then, the effects of parents and parent substitutes during infancy and early childhood have already left imprints on the personalities of those in their care. Later parent figures have a different impact on development.

Praise for Being You

We all need some authority-figures who encourage us to make healthy decisions and reinforce these decisions with positive affirmations. An *affirmation* is a firmly declared opinion that reveals an underlying positive value: "You are important just because you are alive" or "You are really lovable and loving" or "You are capable of great achievements."

As children grow and develop, they can hear many affirmations. The most positive and common affirmations are for being alive and for achieving certain goals parents and teachers consider important. Usually, affirmations are verbal; occasionally, they are nonverbal, coming in the form of a smile or a pat on the back.

> *"Nothing great is ever achieved without enthusiasm."*
> *—Ralph Waldo Emerson*

Good athletic coaches are able to give the kind of affirmations that create the desire in others to try harder to succeed at the highest possible level. A positive new parent figure can do the same.

Motivating Oneself for Self-reparenting

The decision to change your life and to seek and accept happiness is not an easy one to make. It is often the result of a crisis, sometimes the result of day-after-day unhappiness and desperation. A person may become physically ill, emotionally distraught, or deeply despairing, and claim, "I can't stand myself any more; I wish I were dead" or "All things considered, I ought to feel like a success, but instead I feel like a failure. There ought to be more to life than this."

This dissatisfaction, unhappiness, physical, or emotional pain often creates the motivation to change. Some people deny their unhappy feelings. They pretend to others and to themselves that they don't have these feelings.

One way to discover whether or not you would feel better by learning how to be a good parent to yourself is to ask yourself these questions:

• How would I be different now if I'd had ideal parents when I was little?

• What would those ideal parents be like?

These two questions reveal the challenge to restructure part of your personality by adding a new parent figure, one that you design for yourself to fit your unique needs. This will encourage you in your "being" as well as your "doing." It will encourage you in playing as well as working, will encourage you in recognizing your lovability as well as your capacity to love. With this kind of new internal parent, you will be free to go out in pursuit of happiness!

When you are engaged in self-reparenting, you may choose to use other people, such as a counselor or psychotherapist, to help you. Or, you may redesign your Parent ego state with the help of an imaginary new parent who will have the qualities of a coach, mentor, and/or teacher.

Only you can determine what needs to be added to your Parent ego state. There are many possible choices. The choices you make need to be based on what it will take to overcome the obstacles that prevent you from being happy; obstacles that you must identify yourself. Since each person is unique, each person has unique needs. For example, persons who have a workaholic parent in the Parent ego state may want to add a new coach type who recommends taking time out for rest, relaxation, and recovery.

People who have had overprotective parents may have difficulty taking risks and may continually expect others to take care of them and make their decisions. They need a new inner Parent who will encourage them to be independent and assertive. When this is accomplished, such people feel much stronger and experience the new Parent as someone inside who is "on their side," but allows them the freedom and ability to take risks.

People who never knew one or both of their parents, or who lost a parent in some way, may experience fear when separated from those they love. They may need a new, reassuring inner-Parent voice that tells them, "No matter what happens to me, my spirit will always be with you."

When the motivation to change is present, the process of self-reparenting can begin.

Previewing the Action Plan

This first chapter is designed to increase your awareness that you may not be as happy as you want to be, that some changes are needed, that something important in life seems to be missing. That "something missing" is an inner Parent who prizes continuing education and strives to keep his or her parenting up-to-date in a rapidly changing world. This Parent encourages clear thinking, freedom, autonomy, and joy within oneself and for sharing with others.

The second chapter is a study of parents in general, of the typical parenting styles, and children's responses to them. This chapter includes exercises for analyzing your own parent figures who, for better or worse, have become part of your personality.

The third chapter allows you to further explore the drama of life, examining particularly what your own inner Child needs and wants currently and the possibilities of reprogramming yourself to get it. The use and abuse of injunctions by parents are discussed, as are the effects of these injunctions on children and the methods children devise to deal with injunctions. Finally, the culture and subcultures in which children are raised have a powerful influence on the development of their personalities and can actually act as parent-figures. This idea of culture as parent-figure is considered.

The fourth chapter will help you clarify how typical parent programming affects creative and logical thinking. Parenting skills and the effects of strong versus weak parenting methods are explored in order to assist you in the self-parenting process employed by your own new inner Parent. How children respond to various parenting skills is an essential element of personality development. You will also consider who might assist you in your self-determined reprogramming process.

The fifth chapter considers the influence of love in our lives, from parents, from other parent figures, from the new parents we design for ourselves, and the consequences of the presence or absence of active love expressions during childhood. The importance of touch, dialogue, and love in the development of the new inner Parent is emphasized.

The sixth chapter points to the various sources of personal power that you are able to mobilize. As with computers, some new programs are better than others, especially those that both provide what we want and need and are designed so we can make them work.

The seventh chapter involves learning the specific techniques for how to make contracts with yourself so that you can achieve that which you need and want to enhance your life in specific ways.

The eighth and final chapter is an invitation to celebrate—to celebrate your newfound courage to pursue happiness for yourself and perhaps help others install new programs so that they too can find what they want for themselves.

If you use this action plan, you'll create a new, loving Parent within, a parent who will treat you with dignity, respect, and care and show you how to give and get the same treatment to and from others. You'll have new hope, new success, new happiness. You'll be on your way. You'll be able to take care of yourself like a good parent would do. You'll be able to coach yourself and act like a fair referee if you experience some internal or external conflict.

Getting Started

Each of the discovery tool exercises in this book is designed to assist you in updating your inner Parent through an action program. You will, for example, learn how to add something to your inner Parent ego state that will be like an enthusiastic coach and will encourage you to perform well, encourage you to take care of your body, and encourage you to continue to improve.

Or, you will learn how to add a mentor who will have many of the same characteristics but a somewhat different style. You will learn which style seems to fit you best.

To get started on the process, take a few moments to do

the exercises that follow. None of them will be "too much work." Some may entice you to reflect at deeper levels about who you are, how you got to be that way, and what you want your life to be in the future.

In each step of the action plan for happiness, you'll be working on "you" and, like a detective or research scientist, you'll be searching for clues that will lead you to a greater understanding of yourself and the many potentials still waiting for you to develop and express. Like putting together a jigsaw puzzle, suddenly you'll find a brightly colored piece of your life that will fall into place and open your mind to the larger pattern of your life. Start now! You can do it!

Discovery Tools

Looking Ahead

Many of the exercises at the end of this and the following chapters suggest that you write out answers to questions or that you jot down your thoughts or plans. You might find it helpful to use a journal of some sort. This could be a simple spiral-bound notebook or one of those fancy blank books available at stationery stores or gift stores.

Imagining Your Ideal Parent

Get into a comfortable position and imagine you are looking at a good-sized TV screen on which the story of your life is being played. Spend a few moments looking very closely at yourself as you are now; then, on a sheet of paper, jot down answers to the following questions and complete the following sentences.

• If I had had ideal parents when I was little, I would now:

　• The ideal parents would have been:

　• They would have acted:

　• As they were neither perfect nor ideal, I need to start learning how to be a positive coach and ask myself:

　• What do I need to say to myself that will encourage me to take the next step?

　• If I die soon, what might be put on my tombstone? Does that please me? Is it good enough?

　• What do I need to begin to do now so that I will be remembered with a positive and powerful statement?

　• Dare I say to myself, "You can do it. Yes, you can do it."

My Personality, Then and Now

The study of personality is fascinating. The study of your own personality can be even more stimulating. To begin such a study, sit back, take a couple of deep breaths, and relax for a moment. Let your memory drift back to when you were a child. See yourself as you once were, in several different situations. Try to hear your words and the tone of your voice when you spoke. Then reflect on the following.

　• What kind of personality do you think you had? For example, was it warm and friendly? Quiet and obedient? Fearful and escapist?

　• Do you think any of your traits were inherited?

　• Why do you think that?

　• What parts of your personality might have developed in response to your situation and experiences in school or in the geographical area and culture in which you lived?

• Why do you think that?

Now consider your current life.

• How is your personality similar to the way you were in childhood?
   • Has it changed? How might people describe you now?
   • Are you satisfied with what you currently feel and think about your personality?

Influences From the Past

As a brief introduction to self-reparenting, think of some of the important people in your childhood. Consider how they tried to parent you. Did they give advice, do things for you, or tell you how you should act or change?

Write out responses to the following.

• Important people to me in my childhood:
• How they acted, or tried to act, as parents to me:
• How this affected me then:
• How it affects me now:
• Do you need more parenting-type people in your current life? If so, why?
• Do you need fewer parenting people in your life? If so, why?
• What kinds of people do you want to have around you? For example, do you want people to listen to you and not interrupt? Do you want people to ask you what you think instead of voicing their own opinions and ignoring yours?

• How and what can you begin to teach or coach yourself so that you can meet those kinds of people?

• What do you need from other people that you could partially or completely fulfill by developing these characteristics in your new inner Parent (who then would function as an encouraging coach and not as a controlling, overprotective, or indifferent parent)?

Affirmations and Action

Again, recall your childhood and adolescence. What kind of affirmations were you given? Were the affirmations given for being the person you were or for doing particular things?

• Did you receive affirmations merely for "being," such as, "I'm so glad you were born."

• From whom?

• Did you receive affirmations for doing, such as, "You did a fine job with your homework?"

• From whom?

Consider the above patterns. Do you need new affirmations for being or doing?

Do you need affirmations so you will feel freer to pursue happiness? If so, what kind of affirmations would you need to give to yourself or hear from others?

A coach might say, "You can learn to do it, so get going." Would that work for you? If so, how about saying it to yourself today—at least 10 times—"You can learn it, so get going"?

2

Expanding Your Options

As a child, did you ever run away from home (or want to run away) because your parents were mean to you?

Do you ever wonder how life would be now if you had had different parents?

Do you ever compare your parents with someone else's and feel ashamed of them, or proud of them?

Do you sometimes feel as if you are still being treated like a child who has not been liberated to grow up?

If so, you need to modify your Parent ego state by adding the type of parent who will interact with the inner Child and Adult parts of your personality so that you can get on with life, liberty, and the pursuit of happiness.

A Look Ahead

In this chapter you will become more aware of positive and negative parenting styles that are commonly used by parental figures. You will also learn more about your potentials for strengthening your own positive attributes. You will learn more about the liberty you have to find ways to raise your expectations from dissatisfaction to high-flying happiness.

With positive instead of negative expectations you can expand current and future options. Negative parenting figures from the past do not need to interfere with personal growth in the present.

You will gain tools for becoming more aware of the positive and negative ways in which you were parented, mentored, and coached. You may find yourself thinking, "Oh, that's why I feel and act certain ways sometimes. My parent figures must have passed that on to me in some way."

Longing for Something More

We all receive something important at birth—our lives. Our bodies might not have been healthy. We might have had poor care or inherited a disease that has limited us. At least we are alive, even if our liberty to enjoy life is sometimes diminished.

> "Let us not look backwards in anger, not forward in fear, but around in awareness."
> —James Thurber

Most people, no matter what they have, or how happy they seem to be, long for something more. This longing is natural. The "more" may be more money, more self-esteem, more friends, or more liberty to pursue happiness and get more out of life.

Even people who have experienced adequate or superior parenting continue to search for something more. The search may lead to a new job in an environment offering the liberty to make choices, such as being allowed to create a flexible work schedule. Or, the search may lead to taking an overdue vacation to recuperate and think about additional options for obtaining more.

What is defined as "more" to one person may mean "nothing" to another. It depends upon the values each holds and how each one defines happiness.

The Value of Dissatisfaction

When people want more of something, or more from someone, it is because they believe it will bring them satisfaction and maybe happiness. The two feelings are not the same.

> "You see things and ask 'Why?' But I dream things that never were and ask "Why Not?'"
> —Thomas Edison

Satisfaction is experienced as quiet pleasure, relief, peace, well-being, or contentment. Needs or desires are gratified, at least for the moment, and the mind, body, and emotions feel in balance.

Happiness is more intense. When happy, the balancing of one's body, thoughts, and emotions may take second place to experiencing excitement and joy.

Feeling satisfied and in balance automatically assists the body in fashioning healthy responses to many kinds of stress.

However, there can be advantages to being dissatisfied. When needs or desires are constantly thwarted—either by other people or by our own internal mechanisms of denial or despair—the awareness and longing for something more may be lost.

This longing can be rediscovered. Dissatisfaction is not the same as hopelessness. When feeling hopeless, people feel trapped. They give up and do not try to change situations.

However, when feeling dissatisfied, they often become strongly motivated to do or change something. If we are dissatisfied with our appearance, we may feel motivated to improve it. If dissatisfied with our lifestyle, we may think about changing it. If dissatisfied with our children, we may question our style of parenting. If dissatisfied with a job, we may want to get out of it. We can learn to say to ourselves, "I can think it over. I can find a way."

To think about expanding our options requires an awareness of our weaknesses, strengths, and potentials. Part of this lies in exploring the attributes and training we received from our parents. Recognizing strengths gives us power to recognize our weaknesses. Recognizing weaknesses can motivate us to change. Recognizing potentials enables us to think about our options and encourage ourselves. We can be like new parents, teachers, tutors, mentors, or coaches to ourselves. This can lead to new heights of happiness.

By learning how to use the Adult ego state so that it can function like a referee if we experience inner conflict, we can evaluate our decisions and pursue new ones. The positive value of disappointment and dissatisfaction is that it can lead to action.

The Desire for Liberty

There is a connection between liberty and happiness that is worth thinking about. Although Patrick Henry (1736–1799) had personal liberty, he wanted more of it for the people of Colonial America. He failed as a storekeeper and farmer. Then he discovered law, educated himself, passed the bar, and became a strong patriot. He also became active in getting some concepts from the Bill of Rights into the Constitution. The rights were designed to protect individual human liberty from interference by others or by the federal government. This helped to affirm the right to pursue happiness.

Once, when speaking before a revolutionary convention, he stated his priorities: "I know not what course others may take but as for me give me liberty or give me death." That was a strong statement and, if actually given the choice, Patrick Henry might have preferred imprisonment to death, but his words were powerful motivators to others.

The symbol for the American promise of the freedom to pursue happiness stands at the entrance to New York harbor. It is the Statue of Liberty. This statue, made of copper and iron, was given to the United States by the French to commemorate self-government and symbolize friendship.

Many children do not experience their parents as friends or as authorities who want them to be free. Instead, parents are often perceived as trying to rule the world by laying down the law and deciding which permissions to give and which to withhold.

Children are particularly alert to restrictions on how they use their time. Like soldiers on leave, they believe liberty leads to happiness. "Wow, I don't have to do any homework tonight and they said I could watch TV. " "Guess what! Mom said I didn't have to clean my room this week." "My dad is letting me stay out much later than he used to."

Of course, freedom to use one's own time does not always lead to happiness. Coaching is often needed. Not being encouraged to complete assigned homework may lead to failing grades at school. Watching TV may lead to boredom or nightmares. Living in dirt or confusion may contribute to feelings of shame or inadequacy. Staying out late may interfere with health and success.

Liberty attained through the actions of others may feel like paradise. People liberated from a prisoner of war camp know this feeling. So do those who are liberated from the fear of a life-threatening illness by the words "You're going to be fine" from a respected physician. In such cases, the patient is likely to first feel relief and then elation. At this moment there is often an attitudinal turning back to the belief, it's never too late to be happy.

In addition to attaining a sense of liberty through the actions of others is the sense of being able to design your own internal freedom. When this is done, no matter how much unhappiness a particular situation may hold, life is experienced as having meaning. Self-reparenting contributes to this development.

Some people liberate themselves without being aware of doing so by adding respected models to their Parent ego states. These models may be fictional or real people. They may have names or be nameless. Discovering who these models might be is an interesting challenge in the process of self-reparenting.

Expanding Your Expectations for Success

Expectations we have of ourselves are greatly influenced by the opinions we formulate about ourselves in childhood. We may think of ourselves as capable in some ways and not in others. When we achieve our positive expectations, we think of ourselves as successful. And, we are.

Success, or "more success," is interpreted differently by different people. Success may be found in a major accomplishment or in a small act. Success to one person could be a new job. To another it could be saving money and buying a new house. Success could also be improved health or improved appearance, improved family life, or friendships. It could be winning a race, flying a kite, gathering a bouquet of flowers, preparing a gourmet meal, singing a song, dancing a dance.

Success takes many forms. Whatever form it takes, people who experience success feel a sense of achievement and, for the moment at least, a measure of happiness.

Some people feel most successful when they have to work hard to overcome major obstacles, like learning how to control a drinking habit or exercising regularly after an illness or injury.

> *"It is a healthy thing, now and then, to hang a question mark on the things you have long taken for granted."*
> *—Bertrand Russell*

Other people view success as coping with specific daily tasks. To these people, getting out of bed, leaving the house, and going to work is success for the day. Coping reasonably well on a daily basis with a physically or emotionally ill family member may be seen as success.

Still other people view success as the achievement of long-range goals such as graduation from college, learning to play the piano, being voted into public office, securing a job promotion, or improving a relationship that is falling apart.

When people hold one view strongly, and value one kind of goal (short-term, long-term, difficult to achieve) while discounting others, they may miss out on happiness. Moments of true success may seem hollow, and some people may feel trapped by circumstances beyond their control or by what they consider their personal failures.

The longing for something more is most fully satisfied in people who see value in achieving daily tasks, value in achieving long-range goals, and value in finding the courage to solve crisis situations.

More or Less at Home

The first sense of self as a success or failure develops within the home, regardless of what the home is like. Some homes are like prisons; some are like sanctuaries. Some are like playgrounds or circuses or hospitals or hotels or schools.

One person might say, "I feel like myself when I'm at home." Someone with the opposite view might retort, "It's only when I'm away from home that I feel like myself."

"Home" is a joyful word if you like your home and the people in it. If not, the word home may elicit negative feelings such as anger, despair, and dread.

The most common reason people are unhappy at home is that, when they were children, their home was not a happy place to be. Home may have been depressing, or a place of unduly hard work or punishment. The parenting they received there was not conducive to a future successful home life.

All homes have an emotional environment; it may be cold or warm, hostile or loving. The people who live there create the climate, and the climate in turn affects the people. More important than size, location, or furniture are the persons who have the power to create a heaven or a hell for themselves and the others.

Some people like their homes, some detest their homes, and still others feel deeply ambivalent. Those who have negative feelings about their homes usually believe something was missing in their homes when they were young and conclude that, as a consequence, something is missing inside of them. Often the missing part is awareness of their livability and their right to be respected. Some struggle for years to fill this void, then give up in despair. Others recognize the problem and decide to design a better home for themselves, one that contributes to success, not failure. Self-reparenting accelerates this process.

> *"Life is like an onion; you peel off one layer at a time and sometimes you weep."*
> —Carl Sandburg

Awareness of having heard childhood threats such as, "Don't you dare make any noise or I'll whip you so hard you won't forget it" motivates some people to create a warm and loving home—very different from what they endured.

Dissatisfaction with a current home environment may also motivate people to make a change. They may raise the window shades to get more sunlight, hang a favorite picture on the wall, throw away the junk they saved, or invite friends in.

Each person has a dream of what home should be like. The dream may be of a convenient apartment in the city, a simple cabin with a scenic view of majestic mountains, a farm with acres of waving wheat or livestock, a house in the suburbs with a picket fence.

The old saying "A man's home is his castle" implies the freedom to live as one chooses. It is a way of saying that people should be in charge of their own lives at home, if nowhere else. It implies that people have the right to rule their private lives, and this rule cannot be breached without loss of happiness.

The issue of who does or should rule a household is often debated. When two or more people vie for dominance, friction erupts. Competitiveness replaces cooperation. Power plays become common. Children may compete for a parent's attention and vice versa. Parents may compete with each other. They may argue, shout, rant, and rave to try to prove their superiority over others in the house.

In a home environment, where cooperation usually leads to happiness, the lack of cooperation often leads to pain. The words "Be it ever so humble, there's no place like home" may be only a dream. However, when using self-reparenting, the longing for something more can motivate you to create a new reality, a happy home. People can actually learn to enjoy their homes, and can also learn to enjoy the liberty of feeling at home in the world.

Typical Parenting Styles

All cultures, through their rules and traditions, give and withhold specific rights to pursue personal happiness, and parent figures are the primary conveyors of these beliefs.

The rationale for developing a new part of your personality and becoming like a good parent, mentor, or coach to yourself is based on the belief that liberation and the pursuit of happiness are possible. It is also based on the trust and knowledge that creating new internalized parent figures can counteract the negative parts of the old ones.

In brief, typical parenting styles that interfere with children's growth toward autonomy include being overly critical, too protective, inconsistent, argumentative, uninvolved, super-organized, or emotionally needy.

Typical parenting styles that contribute to children's growth include being reasonable, encouraging, consistent, peacemaking, caring, relaxed, and responsible.

Overly critical parents say such things as "You're stupid and you'll never amount to anything" or "Can't you ever do anything right?" or "Get lost." When operating in the Parent ego state of their personality, people who had overly critical parents will use these same words to themselves or others, or embody them in nonverbal behavior.

A positive, affirmative style is used by *reasonable parents*. They may be authoritarian in their opinions, but they do not make unreasonable demands or criticize in ways that are sarcastic or vicious.

Overly protective parents say such things as "I'll drive you whenever it rains," "Let me do it for you," "Don't worry, I'll take care of everything," or "Now you just tell me if those kids are mean to you." When in the Parent part of the personality, persons who had overly protective parents will act syrupy or overnurturing and interfere with the freedom of others to think for themselves. They often give unwanted advice to other adults as well as to children.

The contrast to this style of parenting is the *encouraging parent* who, like a supportive coach, gives appropriate training and challenges his or her charges to take acceptable risks.

Inconsistent parents say one thing one day and something different the next. On a Tuesday such a parent may say "I worry about you. You must come home on time" and on Wednesday, say "I don't care what you do, just leave me alone." When in the Parent part of their personality, persons who have had inconsistent parents will act similarly, vacillating in what they expect from others.

Clearly, the opposite style of the inconsistent parent is the *consistent parent* who acts in predictable, positive ways and is thought of by others as trustworthy and dependable.

Argumentative parents often disagree with others about many issues. Their arguments may be loud, even vituperative, or filled with sarcasm that leads to further arguments or violence. Arguments may arise over work, education, money, leisure time, sex and sex roles, how to rear children, or just about anything. Each parent may take a strong opposing view, such as "Religion is important and what I believe is right" versus "You're wrong; you don't know what you're talking about."

The opposite of this negative parenting style is the *peacemaking* style. People using this style do not always agree but usually try some form of negotiation. If that is not possible, they recognize the fact that others are entitled to different points of view.

Uninvolved parents are those who may be absent from home a lot. When at home, they don't listen, nor do they share their feelings and thoughts. They may isolate themselves in a particular room or activity and give out the message in one way or another, "Don't bother me, I'm busy." They may also act like the proverbial absentminded professor, forgetting birthdays and other special occasions.

The opposite style is demonstrated by the *caring parent* who may not always be at home and physically available, yet shows caring in other ways. These parents try to participate in some of their children's activities. They pay attention, really listen, and seldom interrupt. Children with this experience are likely to become independent and feel liberated to think and act for themselves.

> *"A teacher affects eternity; he can never tell where his influence stops."*
> —*Henry Brooks Adams*

Overorganized parents want everything to be perfect. They may clean the house or process data continually and rarely show human, childlike warmth and impulsiveness. Furthermore, they spend so much time getting perfectly organized that they seldom show flexibility. Children with this experience often become rebellious or feel like failures.

The positive side of this parenting style is the *relaxed parent* who also expects high achievement and firmly trains children in tasks such as getting homework done on time, yet does it in a patient rather than a rigid manner.

Emotionally needy parents continually expect to be babied and taken care of or expect to be cheered up and made happy or expect to be criticized and then forgiven. Such parents often manipulate their children into taking parental roles at home. When children of these parents are operating in the Parent ego state, they act in similar ways and express similar emotional needs.

On the opposite side of emotionally needy parents are *responsible parents* who do not wish to burden others with their problems. They take good care of themselves and, like good teachers, are able to offer guidance to others.

The Issue of Control

When thinking about your own parents and other parent figures, it is often useful to consider how they tried to control you and how you tried to control them.

Some parents control their children with criticism or brutality, some with overprotection or with martyr-like complaints such as "You caused me so much pain and grief" or "If you loved me, you would…"

Some parents avoid taking control because they want to avoid responsibility and can blame others when things go wrong, "It's not my fault; it's not my responsibility." Some parents are often overly involved in their own personal interests and complain that they do not have time to handle the parenting requirements.

Parents who are truly disinterested, emotionally disturbed, alcoholic, or severely disorganized, often lack self-control and ignore guidelines that are needed for reasonable and healthy control of children.

As a result, children may be injured in body, mind, or spirit, or develop their own patterns of avoiding control of themselves. When grown up, they may indulge themselves financially as well as in other ways. They allow other people to take advantage of them because they do not know how to set limits for themselves or establish boundaries with others. The models they had in childhood were inadequate.

As you think about parenting figures in your life, you may conclude that you had too much negative parenting.

Or, you may have had positive parenting in some areas of your life and not in others. If so, you may feel that something important was missing, or that something was out of balance.

In any case, you probably wished for something more, someone who would encourage you to succeed more fully. This would be an ideal new parent, mentor or coach to add to your Parent ego state. This Parent could guide you and love you in your pursuit of happiness. As you discover more about the parents of your past, and what you need for now and the future, you can create this new part of your personality. Take time to do it.

Discovery Tools

More for Me
Consider what you wanted more of when you were a child. Did you want more peace in the family and less turmoil? More safety from a parent who could be violent? More attention to you as a person? More compliments when you succeeded? On a sheet of paper write answers to the questions below or complete the following statements:

- During preschool years, I wanted more:
- During early school years, I wanted more:
- During high school, I wanted more:
- During young adult years, I wanted more:
- Since then, I have wanted more:
- If these physical and/or emotional needs had been met, how would your life be different?

No Place Like Home

Put yourself in a comfortable position. Relax any tension you may experience in your body. Then turn on an imaginary TV set and switch the dials until pictures of the places you lived when you were young begin to form on the screen in front of you.

Look carefully at yourself in each of your "homes" and observe how your sense of self is forming your feelings of success or failure.

• What word (such as prison or sanctuary) would you use to describe each home you have lived in?

• Who is ruling where you live? Do children sometimes rule, perhaps when the ruler is away? Is there a crown prince or princess? Are there slaves or servants? Who plays these roles? How were they chosen?

• Are family members satisfied or dissatisfied with the ruler and the rules? Does the rule change hands? If so, why, and what happens next?

Success and Failure in Childhood

Get into a comfortable position. Let your memory drift back to childhood situations when you experienced success or failure, then contemplate responses to the following.

• How old were you? How did you feel?

• What did you think?

• How did your parent figures, your teachers, mentors, or coaches respond to your successes and failures? Were they critical, applauding, or indifferent?

- An example of a success I experienced was when I:
- Others responded to me with:
- A situation where I felt like a failure was:
- Others responded to me with:

As you review some of your childhood successes and failures, does a pattern emerge?

- Were your successes generally in school?
- In sports?
- In friendships?
- In hobbies?
- In something else?
- Were your failures in a specific field?
- Are these clues to what you now need to restructure part of your personality?

Negative Parenting Styles

All parents are unique in the details of how they parent. Yet, there are some general parenting styles. Your parents and parent substitutes probably acted in both positive and negative ways. This exercise is designed for you to become aware of some of the negatives you experienced at home, school, or in the neighborhood in which you grew up.

Which parent figure showed a particularly negative parenting style? How? What was your response?

- Overcritical?
- Overprotective?
- Inconsistent?

- Argumentative?
- Uninvolved?
- Super-organized?
- Emotionally needy?

Positive Parenting Styles

Positive parenting styles are the opposite of those in the previous exercise. For example, the parent who is reasonable and supportive is the opposite of the overcritical parent. The parent who is able to compromise, negotiate, and make peace is the opposite of the parent who continually argues and fights. What were the positives in your parents?

Which parent showed a positive parenting style? How? What was your response?

- Reasonable?
- Encouraging?
- Consistent?
- Peacemaking?
- Caring?
- Relaxed?
- Responsible?

Owning Your Successes

Many people easily remember their failures but forget their successes, such as receiving good grades in school, managing a difficult job, or coping with a critical illness. They may not compliment themselves for breaking a bad habit or for learning how to use money and time responsibly. They may "forget" how they overcame fear of people by going to a class or joining a club or singing in a choir. Thinking of themselves as failures, they deny their successes. This exercise is meant to allow you to "own up" and accept your successes as valid. On a separate piece of paper or in a page of your journal or notebook, list as many items as you can think for each of the following:

- My successes in daily tasks and short-term goals
- My successes with long-term goals
- My successes in overcoming major obstacles

To what do you attribute your successes?

Expanding Your Options

To add to your new and developing Parent ego state, review the section on positive parenting styles, then do the following:

- Select three of the parenting style options that would be positive in your life and explain to yourself why you selected each.
- Select a positive parenting style and use it on yourself for an entire week.
- Ask a real or imaginary coach about the best ways to create and enforce rules and listen to the response.
- Ask a real or imaginary teacher or mentor how life would be similar or different if you expand your parenting options in positive ways.

3

Recognizing the Need for Self-Reparenting

Did you ever decide that you would never be like your parents, no matter what?

Have you ever caught yourself speaking or doing something negative just as they once did?

Did you want to be like one of your parents but not like the other, only to discover you had some of the disliked parent's traits?

Who were your other parent figures and how did they act to influence you?

The first step to self-reparenting was to get acquainted with the transactional analysis theory of personality and how it can be used for your benefit. The second step was to increase your awareness that parents, teachers, and others in similar roles are less than perfect. Your parent figures may or may not have wanted you to have life, liberty, or the determination to pursue happiness, or perhaps they were simply indifferent to your needs for these things. But you are alive and have succeeded in many ways.

A Look Ahead

Have you ever noticed that people, including parents, sometimes change? And, that sometimes they change for the better? If so, you are ready to highlight the Parent part of your personality more directly so you can begin to change what you want to change.

Reparenting yourself, by adding new qualities to your Parent ego state, will put you on a new path to freedom. In this step of the process, you will analyze your particular parent figures in order to clarify how you were influenced by them in ways that could interfere with your liberty and your pursuit of happiness.

Change Is a Process

Throughout life our bodies change. In youth, the changes lead to increased strength and development. With aging, the changes often lead to decreased strength. Granted, to some degree, the health and development of our bodies are influenced by genetics. But they are also influenced by accidents, illnesses, and nutrition. Currently there is a widespread and growing cultural awareness of the influence of exercise. Exercise is used to increase bodily well-being and to restructure parts of the body.

There is less awareness that personality structure and restructuring may involve a similar cycle. Some personality traits seem to be genetically determined. Yet it is also clear that personality can be changed through traumatic experiences or training or the daily conditioning that people experience in their homes, schools, workplaces and neighborhoods.

One of the purposes of this program is to show how personality can also change when people decide for themselves that they want to be different. Instead of being fearful and withdrawn, a person may decide to be courageous and outgoing. Instead of acting like a loser, a person may decide to become a winner. Instead of expressing rage and anger in destructive ways, a person may convert energy into channels that lead to success. Instead of feeling inadequate or stupid, a person may change this self-image and build a personality grounded in higher self-esteem.

The process is a little like bodybuilding. First, you determine the weaknesses, then establish the goal. A plan of action comes next. As the plan is implemented, you continu-

> *"Let me tell you a secret that has led me to my goal. My strength lies solely in my tenacity."*
> —*Louis Pasteur*

ally evaluate results so that necessary adjustments can be made as you go. Evaluation of bodybuilding includes testing of muscles. Evaluation of personality change is more subtle and subjective, but a sense of expanded awareness and greater satisfaction often points to positive personality change.

When people experience positive new changes, they get excited and want more. Then the *process* of personal growth becomes as important as the outcome. All of life is a change process. Self-reparenting, the art of learning how to be a good parent to yourself, facilitates positive change.

Life as a Drama

Shakespeare wrote that all the world is a stage and that we are the players on it. From prologue to final curtain, we play roles. These roles are parts of psychological scripts that have all the components of dramas played out on theatrical stages.

Without a written script in our hands, we often act as we were once directed to do or as we have chosen to do. The roles may be obvious or played in a subtle manner. When the obvious shows, we may be accused of "putting on an act." Less obvious negative roles may be so hidden that others imagine only the positive about us and assume that's the way we really are.

Script themes tend to be constructive, destructive, or going nowhere. People with positive constructive scripts reflect a belief that life is worthwhile and has meaning. They are willing to work for what they want and make the best out of negative situations.

Those who live by destructive scripts do not respect themselves or others. They may express such negative behavior that they become suicidal or homicidal. Children under parental authorities who have destructive scripts tend to withdraw when it is possible to do so because of the natural fear they experience when such people act out their rage.

Those with going nowhere scripts seldom set positive goals. They tend to live in a banal manner as if nothing really matters. Procrastinating is often a reflection of this and may have come from a parental negative judgement, "You'll never amount to anything."

Each of us "writes" our own scripts although we usually do so under the direction of parents or other authorities. Three most common script roles are Victim, Persecutor, and Rescuer, and we may switch roles in different situations. Children who are victims of parental rage at home may victimize others on the school ground, or they may try to rescue others in ways that reflect positive characteristics of parent figures whom they observed but who were not their biological parents.

The first shaping of a script takes place even before a child is born. Genetic inheritance, the health of the parents, and their attitudes toward the coming birth are strong factors in determining the stage and setting on which the curtain finally rises.

After that, regardless of who is directing the situation, the newborn child begins to be programmed to act in certain ways.

> *"Truth burns up error."*
> *—Sojourner Truth*

In a life drama, the curtain on Act I often falls during adolescence. By then, the roles to be played and the lines to be spoken have been learned. The learning will have taken place at home, school, out in the community, or in some combination of all of these places. Usually, the original director of a life drama is a parent figure who also manages to get onto the stage in one way or another.

The curtain on Act II usually goes up when people living by the script partly written by others, are in their late teens or early twenties. Many feel stuck in their roles, others begin to ask themselves the question, "If I go on as I now am, what will happen during the next act or when the final curtain falls?"

This is a basic question that we need to ask ourselves time and time again. It brings our roles and the consistent behavioral patterns known as personality into awareness so that we can see that we are living parts of our lives by scripts that can be rewritten toward goals of freedom and happiness.

Family Loyalty

Loyalty to parents or family usually begins when children internalize parental values and expectations whether positive or negative, and do so without awareness. If they break away from the values and think and act independently, they often feel they have betrayed family loyalty and, as a result, feel guilty—even when these independent values and thoughts take the form of authentic growth and success.

Of course, many families encourage growth and success. The loyalty of a family's members may be based on happy shared experiences, or successfully coping with a crisis, or authentic expressions of love. However, many children develop loyalty to the family because they are coerced: "Don't you dare tell anyone or you won't be able to play outside for a month." Later, the bond of loyalty may become a ball-and-chain, seriously restricting thinking, feeling, and behavior.

Because young children are so much under the authority of their parents, they are often unaware that the demands for family loyalty may be unjust. Parents who elicit promises from their children for lifetime care create an unjust family loyalty. Children who promise often feel guilty and angry if they become aware that the demand is unjust. Parents also create an unfair family loyalty if they threaten or otherwise manipulate children not to tell anyone about the parents' failings. Trying to keep family secrets can be an impossible obligation.

Isn't it strange that children of any age usually expect their parents to be loyal to them no matter how the children may mess up their own lives. Parents seem to have similar expectations. When this kind of obligation becomes too great a burden, the relationship often breaks down, sometimes beyond repair.

The Internalized Parents

Some children are reared by both of their biological parents, some by only one. Some are reared by grandparents or foster parents or stepparents. Some are parented by older siblings or nursemaids. Some grow up in institutions where the staff serves as parents.

In any case, these parenting figures are internalized in childhood and become the Parent part of the personality. This Parent part functions in two ways: externally toward other people and internally toward oneself (especially toward the inner Child).

Most people have more than one parent figure, and their internalized parents may not agree with each other. The result is confusion. For example, one parent may believe religion is important; another parent may strongly disagree. As a result, their children may become ambivalent or take sides against one of the parents or have conflicting internal feelings which may become painful.

Another kind of parent that confuses children is the one who gives conflicting messages at the same time, or inconsistent messages at various times, like "Come close to me" and "Stay away and don't bother me." Other parents may be critical one moment and overly indulgent the next. This also confuses children, who need stability in their lives. As they grow up, they fluctuate between being self-critical and self-indulgent. And so it goes.

Parents who have internalized a belief in their own superiority may be highly critical of others and feel self-righteous about their own values and lifestyles. One of the most important steps in self-reparenting is to analyze the parent figures of childhood and discover how they are still functioning within you, whether you have been aware of it or not.

Using the discovery tools at the end of this chapter, you will be able to explore both the positive and negative aspects. Some people avoid looking at anything positive because they are so angry at some of the negative things their parents did to them. When they refuse to look at the positive, they deny themselves an important source of strength. This source of strength could be used productively in spite of some other attributes of their parent figures that are counterproductive.

Some people act and feel as if they were stuck and consequently are not happy. They harbor so much resentment against their parents that they refuse to admit their parents had any positive attributes at all. They don't want the facts. "I've made up my mind and I'm not going to change it no matter what!" They refuse to examine possible extenuating circumstances for their parents' negative parenting. Other people don't want to evaluate their parents even if their parents were very good, because they think evaluations are disloyal or disrespectful.

People who have been brutalized, sexually molested, or deserted by their parents often find it difficult to recognize anything positive in their parents. In such cases, an awareness that some of their own positive intelligence and appearance was directly inherited from their parents' genes helps build new self-esteem (and some appreciation for their parents).

When people discover that there were some positive things about their parents despite what may have been parent pathology, they often experience more self-esteem. "Well, my mother was crazy as anything," claimed one woman, "but she sure was a good cook." "My father didn't know how to get along with people, even himself. But he worked hard to support us," affirmed a man who was analyzing his parents' positive and negative attributes.

> *"There are no illegitimate children, only illegitimate parents."*
> —Thomas Jefferson

Eventually, through self-analysis and through actively reexamining their childhood, most people can come to terms with their imperfect, yet understandable, parents. They let go of much of their resentment and sometimes even forgive their parents. They also let go of the unrealistic belief that if their parents had only been perfect, life now would be perfect. They are in a good position to create a new Parent that will reinforce their growing independence and cheer for them enthusiastically in the pursuit of happiness.

Parental Injunctions

All children receive messages or injunctions about their worth from their parents, including foster parents, grandparents, older siblings, and other family members, as well as teachers and people who live in the neighborhood. Any or all of these messages contribute to a child's positive or negative esteem.

A child who receives only positive messages will have much less need later in life for self-reparenting than one with the opposite experience. However, even if a child has ideal parents, there are often other significant persons, such as teachers, stepparents, grandparents, or older siblings, who give injunctions that interfere with health and happiness.

Injunctions are commands, directives, or orders. The word is used here to refer to statements or acts by parenting figures that adversely affect a child's sense of being alive and well, capable and competent, free and joyful.

There are a number of basic negative injunctions, according to psychotherapists Mary and Bob Goulding. The first two are against the very idea of *being* itself: "Don't be" and "Don't be you." Two are about relationships: "Don't be close" and "Don't belong." Next are those concerned with personal growth: "Don't grow up" and "Don't be a child." Others are against physical or emotional wellness: "Don't be well" and "Don't be sane." Two are against achievement: "Don't be important" and "Don't succeed."

Don't Be is often a lethal injunction. It is a message given verbally or nonverbally by parents who do not want a particular child to exist. This can be for many reasons. The parents may be very young, unmarried, and unable to cope with the problems involved in having and raising a child. Or, they may believe they already have enough or too many children and not want "one more mouth to feed" or "one more diaper to change." Other parents may be physically or emotionally ill, almost incapable of coping with life at all. Still other parents may dislike each other intensely and see a child as a burden that could put pressure on them to stay together. Then there are an increasing number who don't want children because children would interfere with their careers. The most common responses to "Don't be" are passivity and depression.

Don't Be You is not as lethal as "Don't be," but it is still a devastating attack on a child's identity. It is most strongly given by parents who wish a child were of the opposite sex. Parents may openly complain, "Oh, if you were only a boy" or "I sure wish you were a girl." The child soon learns that his or her basic sexual identity does not please his or her parents.

> "The unexamined life is not worth living."
> —Plato

Children may even be dressed and treated as if they were of the opposite sex. This often causes deep despair or confusion, and liberation from it may require extensive professional help.

Don't Be Close is a negative injunction often given by parents who see themselves as too busy to listen, comfort, play with, or teach a child. This injunction is also given nonverbally by parents who abandon their children. A child who is abandoned may decide never to love again, or never to be close to a person of the same sex as the parent who left. A child may make a similar decision if a parent dies. Death feels like abandonment.

Another way this injunction is experienced is when divorce, or continuing conflict, splinters a family. When strong bitterness is expressed between parents, they may compete for the affection of a child and issue the message, "Don't be close to that so-and-so of an ex-spouse; only be close to me."

Don't Belong is experienced by children if they are rejected by parents who wish a particular child were not part of the family—often because of embarrassment over physical or emotional problems that the child might possess. In such cases, it is not unusual for a child to wish for other parents.

Furthermore, if children are taught that they are better than others, or not as good as others, they may also feel like outsiders. And, if they are rejected by their peers or by teachers, they may also feel like they don't belong anywhere.

Don't Grow Up is an unspoken command of parents who want their children to remain under their control. In spite of what they may claim, such parents do not want their children to think or act independently. They want obedience and compliance to their opinions, ideas, and demands. They criticize with remarks such as, "Can't you grow up and think like a decent human being?" These parents are really reinforcing the idea in their children's minds that they are, in fact, destined to remain perpetual children—exactly what the parents wish for them to be.

Don't Be a Child is just the opposite injunction of "Don't grow up." It is often given by parents who themselves act like children. They reverse the parent-child roles and insist that their children care for them—either physically or psychologically or both. It is also given by parents who are overly ambitious for their children. Pushing their children to be first, such parents may feel inadequate and use their children as compensation for what they lack in themselves.

The same message often accompanies a "Don't be close" injunction given by parents who are too busy and refuse to listen to what they label as "kid stuff." The same message comes through if they never play with their children or imply that play is less important than work.

Don't Be Well is a very subtle injunction given by parents who, often without awareness, expect a child to be physically dependent upon them, although it may not be necessary. After all, if a child is not well, then a parent's attention is required. This can lead to a parent feeling important and necessary. In a family where a sibling or other family member is chronically ill or incapacitated in some way, it is not unusual for a healthy child to feel a twinge of guilt for being well.

Don't Be Sane is an injunction sometimes given by parents who do not want their children to be sane because they might see how irrational they, the parents, are. It is also given with accusations between two parent figures when they make remarks to each other such as, "You're impossible; you're always acting crazy" or "Everybody in your family is crazy." The implication is that some form of insanity has been inherited or is acceptable.

Don't Succeed is an injunction that often leads to a banal script. It can come from parents who do not know how to cope with success, or from siblings who manage to downplay success, or from a teacher who may have a classroom favorite. Often the message voiced in the home is "You think you're better than your own family, don't you."

Such parent figures can give the injunction by continually criticizing less-than-perfect grades so that a child concludes "I'm not perfect; therefore, I can't succeed." When grown up, these persons may almost reach goals, then do something at the last minute that undermines their confidence and stops them from attaining what they want or need.

Don't Be Important is very similar to "don't succeed." To be important is to be special and to be recognized as such. Children with a "Don't be" or "Don't be you" injunction also believe they are not important as individuals.

> *"The supreme happiness of life is the conviction that we are loved."*
> —Victor Hugo

Their parents may pay more attention to another child, a job, or a hobby, and use comments such as "Don't bother me" or "Don't be such a nuisance" or "Don't be a show-off; you're no better than anyone else." They structure their time and interactions in such a way that their children conclude "My needs are not important; therefore, I'm not important."

Don't. . . is a more generalized injunction. It is given in a threatening tone of voice and intended to create paralyzing fear. "Don't you dare look at me like that" or "Don't contradict me or I'll beat you until you wish you were dead."

People who receive this kind of injunction are continually fearful of taking an assertive position, of sticking up for themselves, of making decisions, of doing something new, of thinking, of changing, of taking charge of their own lives. Indeed, of everything.

Escaping from Injunctions

Injunctions can be perceived as realistic or not realistic.

When they are believed to be real, a person may decide "That's the way I am" ("I don't belong") or "That's the way I shouldn't be" ("I shouldn't be important"). These beliefs about oneself can be very damaging, and a child may decide "I can't ever change. I'm hopeless." When this is the case, an outside rescuer, in the form of caring, intelligent adult friend, mentor, or teacher may be needed who will help the person escape from the deadening injunctions.

However, children sometimes perceive the injunctions to be unfair, inaccurate, or grossly exaggerated. When this is the case, they may make a healthy decision: "I don't believe what my parents wanted me to believe about myself" and "I can rescue myself if I have to." The capacity to seek out people who are willing to throw out a lifeline when life or liberty are threatened is part of self-reparenting. So too, is the capacity to throw out a lifeline to one's inner Child who may be feeling as if drowning in a flood of injunctions. By developing a powerful new inner Parent ego state who is potent and protective in emergencies, we can retrain ourselves and escape from all kinds of negative injunctions.

When Cultures Act as Parents

In many ways, cultures and subcultures act like parents. Cultures may be national, racial, or ethnic. Your school, your religion, and your neighborhood are subcultures. There are many more. Each tries to dictate what people are supposed to do or not do. Often mottoes or repetitive phrases reinforce cultural beliefs. Compliance or lack of compliance with these rules determines whether or not a person fits in.

The problem of fitting in is often experienced by children who move from one school to another or by families who move from one part of a country to another. Their life styles and manners may be so different from those in the new situation that they feel like overly critical parents or rejected children. This is changing with the recognition that we live in a multicultural world that has many advantages over parochialism.

Culture shock can be painful or pleasurable, as any traveler knows. Culture shock happens when change is so extreme or rapid that people feel disoriented and out of place. They don't yet fit into the new scene. They may hear a different language spoken, notice different expectations, come up against different laws. Suddenly, in addition to their own parents and their past "cultural parent," they have a new cultural parent to cope with.

The same feelings of shock and stress are often experienced when even minor geographical moves are undertaken. For example, transferring from one school to another can be very traumatic if the school culture is different. So can a move from a rural area to a big city, or vice versa. Also, what may seem like a minor move to parents could be a major move to children.

Being of a particular race, religion, class, or ethnic group in a city where the majority of people are different may also lead to confusion or unhappiness. Being part of a dominant group is usually more comfortable than the opposite. Those of the majority often have more opportunities to pursue life, liberty and personal happiness.

People who immigrate to new countries often experience prejudice. Their previous expectations and lifestyles may not fit into their new life. Some adjust. Others do not.

They may be apprehensive or critical of new ways and experience despair, or they may be pushy and try to influence others to accept the values they brought with them. They may be ridiculed, ignored, or discriminated against in life-threatening ways. Jobs may be hard to get, language barriers overwhelming, and the new country that was expected to be a liberating home may instead be a confusing, even restricting, one.

In spite of this, the search for happiness goes on. Many continue their old customs and form new subcultures of like-minded people. Others adjust to the new culture either happily or unhappily, depending on many variables and on comparisons made to "the way it was back home." Gradually the culture shock disappears.

New Power for Change

As you discover the complexities of the parent figures that you internalized, you may from time to time feel either trapped or freed. Perhaps the parents of your past would encourage you to change; perhaps they would fight against change, or undermine your change in some less direct way: "Oh, you don't really want that. You know you don't."

Old Parent messages are powerful. However, new Parent messages can be more powerful if you construct them carefully. After all, the new ones will be more nearly what your inner Child needs to hear. The new messages will help to create a loving-parent-and-happy-child alliance that can overcome the old master-parent-and-child-serf combination. Designing new messages that are acceptable and life-enhancing may seem difficult, but you can do it. You can restructure the Parent part of your personality so that you feel hopeful and powerful, and you can use your hope and power to further liberate yourself for happiness.

Discovery Tools

Are You in Charge?

People change in many ways. Sometimes changes are forced upon them because of circumstances. Sometimes changes just seem to happen without planning. Sometimes we want to change, make a plan to change, and actually do change. Make a list of some of the changes in your life and indicate next to each entry if that change was:

- A change that was forced
- A change that just happened
- A change you planned

Knowing you can change and being able to develop clear plans for change is a sign that you are in charge. What changes do you want to make but have not made yet? What excuses do you use for not making these changes?

The Tyranny of the Shoulds

Many people live under what has been called "the tyranny of the shoulds." They think they should do this, they should do that. A common "should" is keeping secrets about parents. People often fantasize that something terrible will happen if they fail to do so.

This exercise will help you get in touch with fantasies

that could interfere with your evaluating the pros and cons of your parents. Protect the image of your parents as much as you like, just be aware of what it was like then and the possible effect on you now. Write out responses, as long or short as you like, to the following.

- The way my parents acted in private:
- Fantasies I had about telling someone about this:
- The effect of keeping or not keeping their secrets:

Another Look at Your Parent Figures

This is one of the most important steps in the entire self-reparenting process. It will help you make some sense out of your parent figures and their influence on you.

In a column on the left side of a sheet of paper, list the major parent figures you had in childhood. Include your biological parents, stepparents, foster parents and any other people (such as older siblings and grandparents) who had responsibility for you. To the right of each name, list both positive and negative attributes for each parent figure.

Owning Up to Your Inner Parent

Many characteristics of the parents and parent figures you once had were incorporated into your personality and became the Parent part of your personality. Which ones do you own up to? Which have you rejected? Write out responses to the following.

- Positive characteristics of my parents that I sometimes use:
- Situations in which I use these positive characteristics:

• Negative characteristics of my parents that I sometimes use:

   • Situations in which I use these negative characteristics:

   • Characteristics of my parents that I rejected and do not use:

   • How, when, and why I made these decisions to be different in some ways from my parents:

Discovering Negative Injunctions

As you work to understand the effect of your parents and substitute parents upon your life, consider the following list of injunctions.

> Don't be you
> Don't belong
> Don't grow up
> Don't be a child
> Don't be well
> Don't be sane
> Don't be important
> Don't be....
> Don't succeed
> Don't....

Make a list of injunctions you received, then note who you received the injunction from and how it affected your life.

If you received any of these injunctions—directly or indirectly—you will need to develop an ideal Parent message to counteract the old negative ones. For each of the "Don'ts" that you identified, rebuild a "Do" in its place.

As a replacement for the "Don'ts" you have experienced, what wording could you record as a new tape that you could play repeatedly to yourself until it is integrated into your personality?

Rescuers You Have Known

For most people, things go wrong from time to time. They may turn to others to rescue them and, if the rescue is forthcoming, they develop hope. Consider how it was for you.

- Situations when I needed rescue:
- Person or persons who rescued me:
- Ways they rescued me:
- Positive effect on my life:

Perhaps when you have seriously needed help and no one has been available, you called upon your own abilities and courage. How has this affected you in the long run?

- Situations when I rescued myself:
- What I did:
- Positive effect on my life:

Roots and Uprooting

Most people feel emotionally rooted in the culture and subculture in which they lived as a child. If they move, they may take the culture with them or be glad to leave it behind. Make four columns across the top of a sheet of paper, and list the following.

- Cultural changes I made:
- From what:
- To what:
- Effect on my life:

Now, for a moment, sit still and let your mind quiet itself. Reflect on the positive values of your various roots and uprootings.

Consider what new changes you want to make that would increase your happiness.

What kind of ideal new Parent do you currently need to develop that will assist you in continuing change and growth or allow you to successfully make the changes that would increase your happiness?

Your Interacting Cultural Parents

Describe several cultures or subcultures, as you have experienced them.

The subcultures may be national, ethnic, geographical, religious, etc. Include a subculture that had, or still has, the most influence in your life. (Some people find their school subculture is crucial to their self-esteem and self-understanding.)

- How I describe my national culture:
  The effect on me is:
- How I describe my family culture:
  The effect on me is:
- How I describe one of my subcultures (i.e., education, church, community, etc.):
  The effect on me is:

Now analyze the strengths and weaknesses of each of these cultures in terms of how it positively or negatively influenced your life.

If you had an ideal parent figure in your life now, what advice would that person give you? What style would that person use? As one of your parents or grandparents? As a fine teacher? A caring mentor? A powerful coach ?

Think about real or imaginary parent figures from various cultures. Would they advise you to pursue happiness? Advise you to become friends with people from other cultures? What do you need to do to update your old Parent ego state so it helps you be happy in today's changing world?

4

Learning to Be Happy

Have you ever proclaimed with confidence "I can do it if I work at it"?

Have you ever complained "I wish somebody would tell me I'm not stupid" or "I wish I liked myself better than I do"?

Do you listen sometimes to your internal critical parent figures and suddenly feel lowered self-esteem or fear?

Do you ever ask a friend "How can I learn to be happy?

If any of the above is so, it's time for more education about what it means to be a good parent and about the way good self-parenting could change your life today. Understanding the positive effects of good parenting is necessary for self-reparenting. With an educational program you design for yourself, you will be clearer on the potency, permission, and protection that you need in your new Parent. You will also see how habitual ways of acting, thinking, and feeling can interfere with your happiness. You may discover that the additional parent figure you are creating for your Parent ego state needs to use tough love with you sometimes and tender love at other times. Both expressions of love can be effective; both can help you in your process of learning to be happy.

A Look Ahead

Most people have little or no structured education in one of the most important tasks they may ever undertake—the task of parenting. Sometimes parenting comes easily because of having had good role models. Often it is very difficult. People tend to assume that good parenting happens naturally. Not so.

To be a good parent, mentor, or coach to oneself and others requires motivation, education, and skills in communicating. Some people have all three qualities, some have one or two, and some have none. Often people want to be good parents but are not educated in the complex parenting, mentoring, and coaching roles required in today's changing society. Parent and parent substitutes who are the most effective are those who recognize their task is tied to helping children learn how to love, how to think, how to work, and how to play. To accomplish these tasks, parents must be powerful and protective, and they must give children permission to find happiness.

Creativity and Logical Thinking

The capacity to think is an important tool that helps liberate people from unhappiness. Developing a new inner Parent involves both creative and logical thinking. Creative thinking includes fantasizing about what an ideal inner Parent could be. Logical thinking involves analyzing old parental figures and deciding what and how to add a new inner Parent to the space filled by flawed parents of the past.

One of the important discoveries made within the past few years is that people use the left and right sides of their brain for different kinds of thinking. The right side is more involved with creative holistic thinking and the left with logical, analytical thinking.

Some people do not trust the potential of their creative thinking and exaggerate the value of being logical. They may view creative thinking as being speculative, lacking precision, or as characteristic of dreamers. They often fail to see that their pride in being logical may really be part of a grandiose fantasy they have designed to enhance their own self-esteem.

> *"A genius is a talented person who does his homework."*
> —*Thomas Edison*

The opposite can also be true. Some people only pride themselves on their creative thoughts. They do not see that ignoring their capacities to think logically is likely to lead to a life that is out of balance.

Both kinds of thinking are valuable. When balancing a checkbook, the logical skill of analyzing costs and expenditures is useful. However, a creative form of budgeting might solve fiscal problems or increase potential savings. Some people obviously do this better than others.

Both logical and creative thinking are influenced by genetic inheritance, childhood conditioning, adult experience, and education. Although it is generally agreed that intelligence is partly genetic, it has also been proven that intelligence can be raised or lowered during a life span. This depends on motivation, skills, and opportunities for growth and development.

Yet some scholars, such as Howard Gardner, believe there are different kinds of intelligence. High intelligence in one area may not mean a person is competent in other ways. Someone with high mathematical intelligence may lack the kind of musical intelligence shown by great musicians or lack the spatial capacities of architects or the mental capacities professional athletes draw upon to accomplish great physical feats.

Furthermore, having so-called high intelligence does not mean a person will usually think logically or will develop constructive plans of action or be concerned with the happiness of others. Some very intelligent people are clever crooks! Others ignore the information they gather because it does not agree with a personal bias. Furthermore, logical thinking may be labeled "illogical" if it does not coincide with cultural norms.

Whether thinking is logical or illogical, positive or negative, it can nevertheless be creative. Creativity is expressed when the person puts together objects, facts, ideas, feelings, or behaviors in new ways. Creative thinkers don't agree with the commonly held belief that if certain things haven't been done, they can't be done. They trust themselves to think for themselves and redecide poor decisions made in the past. They certainly don't agree with the belief that parents have the sole right to determine their children's future simply because they have done so throughout the years in many cultures.

Fieldwork on Parenting

One of the most effective ways to develop a new Parent is to do "fieldwork" on actual parenting. You actually go out into the field (the community or the real world) to observe methods of parenting and determine how they can be improved. An internship or apprenticeship, where a person is actually doing work under supervision, could be called field work. Many professions require this as part of their training.

In previous generations, apprenticeship or internship in parenting was common. Large families and relatively stable neighborhoods enabled people to observe parenting and decide whether it was adequate or not. Today families are smaller and many people have less time for

> *"It is much easier to be critical than to be correct."*
> —*Benjamin Disraeli*

parenting because they are juggling priorities. Traditional parent education, intrinsic in most cultures, is disappearing today. Because of this, people who are reparenting themselves may know very little about being a parent. That is where the parenting fieldwork comes in. It begins with planned observation.

Planned observation includes going to places where people are parenting young children and observing what is going on—both positive and negative. Supermarkets or department stores are rich fields for observation. Sometimes the parents are harried and the children look hurried, helpless, and hopeless. Sometimes both look happy. Nursery schools and playgrounds reveal a more structured facet of child rearing that involves directed play. This kind of observation can be very useful if you want to be a better new Parent to yourself.

Another way to further understand how to develop your

new Parent is to read books on child development, particularly on developing a child's self-esteem. Throughout your study, ask yourself "What am I learning that is new and positive that I could begin to apply to myself?" "What kind of parenting education do I need that will enhance my ability to be happy?"

The Three Ps in Parent Education

Some people find parenting to be relatively easy, even enjoyable. Some do not. Your parents may have found parenting difficult and frustrating. If so, they probably lacked one or more of the qualities needed to be good parents. Good parents have three basic qualities that people need to have in the new Parent they create for themselves. These basics are potency, protection, and permission.

Potency is strength. A potent parent is strong in the face of adversity or tragedy, strong when meeting difficult commitments or long-term goals. Being strong does not mean denying or repressing unhappy feelings that may be present. It means going ahead with life in spite of difficulty or negative experiences.

Sometimes going ahead takes courage because there may be a risk of failure. The potent person recognizes this possibility and strives to minimize the risk. He or she also recognizes personal feelings of ambivalence, confusion, or fear and owns up to having them. Owning up to having feelings is not the same as being owned by the feelings. Potent persons are in charge of their own feelings and behavior and they know it. Potent persons also are aware of their belief systems and free to change them when it seems like a good idea.

In self-reparenting, the positive new Parent needs to be more potent than the original parents. If not, the old negative messages may continue to be replayed and the inner Child will continue to listen. A strong new Parent will not allow that to happen or will intervene if it starts to occur. An example of healthy intervention is a parent who turns off the TV if a child is watching an inappropriate program. The potent Parent stops the tape from running or, at least, plays a more positive one that drowns out the noise of the past. When the potent new Parent intervenes to cut off old negative tapes, the Child is protected.

Protection is needed by children in order to feel safe and secure. Without protection they usually become fearful adults who are afraid to risk new ventures and afraid to change old patterns of responses. Or, they become adults who do not trust others and frequently attack or defend against real or imagined insults.

Protection can be given to the inner Child in many ways. The new Parent, for example, may encourage the learning of martial arts to someone who is afraid of being physically attacked or encourage assertiveness in the face of criticism. Some people who have had indifferent or overly indulgent parents feel insecure and in need of protection because reasonable limits were not established for them as children. Perhaps their parents failed to provide curfews, or allowed them to make too many choices for themselves—whether to stay in school or drop out, whether to go to bed or stay up late, and so forth. The effect on children is that they may feel powerless and lack a sense of direction.

The person developing a new Parent needs to decide on reasonable limits that are protective and contribute to an inner security. A new Parent can insist on proper health care—food, exercise, decent living conditions, and work habits. When people feel protected by potent internal or external Parent figures, they then feel as if they have permission to succeed.

> *"None can make you feel inferior without your consent."*
> —*Eleanor Roosevelt*

Permission is consent or authorization. It can be given verbally, as in "I think it's great you want to learn something new." A statement such as this encourages a person to learn and be creative. Permission can also be given nonverbally, as with a pat on the back or a warm smile.

People who are frequently depressed or who feel miserable in some other way or who are self-punitive or punitive against others need the permission from an encouraging Parent to break free of this negative cycle. Other people, who neither succeed nor fail, live lives of boredom or trivia. They also need permission to turn around and pursue a different road that may lead to happiness.

Teachers as Parents

Teachers often serve as substitute parents and are incorporated into the Parent ego state much as the parents once were. They, too, may give or withhold their potency, protection, and permissions.

By their very position, teachers also teach the basic curriculum for living and in the process contribute to the personality development of children, often in very positive ways. They show what it is to love by teaching cooperation. They demonstrate what it is to think by teaching problem solving and research skills. They model what it is to work by teaching how to study and complete assignments. They encourage play by teaching children how to enjoy recess and sports. They assist the shy child to become involved and the bully to assume self-control instead of trying to control others.

Teachers who inspire the pursuit of happiness may compensate to some extent if a student's home life is miserable. It is not unusual for some students to idolize and incorporate as parent figures those teachers who treat them with respect and encourage their personal as well as intellectual growth.

Sometimes teachers aren't so nice, or they play favorites. Their method of teaching and learning may be too restrictive: "Keep your feet flat on the floor, your eyes on your books, and no talking or you will stay after school!" They may discourage children from socializing or banding together out of their own fear of losing control over their students. Other teachers don't make time for the less-than-perfect students. They don't provide the special motivation or help that many children need. Learning can become a dreaded chore. Too much control or not enough help can decrease children's self-esteem. The child may decide, "I'm stupid. I can't think, and I'll never amount to anything."

People who make decisions like "I'm stupid" often become very unhappy. Instead of finding learning easy, or at least interesting, they find the whole process of education more and more difficult. This pattern may continue throughout life so that, even on the job, learning something new is painful.

When we are adults, teachers often come to represent internal authority—the "little voice in the back of our head" who keeps us in line or makes us do the chores or finish the assignment or keep our promises. Sometimes we need this admonishment to do what's best. If our teachers have had a positive influence, the internal teacher will be a gentle reminder. If we had unhappy experiences in school, we may be very hard on ourselves. We need to learn to be good teachers to ourselves.

A Curriculum for Parenting

Teaching well usually involves knowledge of the subject, interest in helping people learn about it, ability to make the subject come alive and to demonstrate how it can be applied. Any school curriculum consists of various courses that are related to each other in an organized way. Parents need to offer their children a similar opportunity for wholeness. Specifically, they need to teach (often by example) how to love, how to think, how to work, and how to play.

How to love is best taught by providing a home where love is present. Love is more than warm feelings, acts of kindness, nurturing, and approval. Love includes setting limits—saying no as well as yes. Love is sometimes challenged when people are tired, anxious, or critical, or when communication is inadequate and conflict erupts. It is also challenged when tragedy strikes in the form of accident, death, or illness. We need love when despair sets in because a job is lost or a friend betrays us or a colleague doesn't keep promises. Love is not just an expression of happiness when things are going well. It includes being present for others when things are not going well.

The need to love oneself is also learned at home. Parents who act like martyrs to their children may believe they are showing love. They are not. They many be overindulging their children who will, in turn, take a self-centered view of life and overindulge themselves. Parents who teach love demonstrate by their actions the importance of taking responsibility for yourself and acting in loving ways because you are lovable.

How to think is best taught by encouraging children to do their own thinking and not giving them all the answers. Parents who want their children to think encourage them to observe the external world as well as their internal thoughts and feelings and to think of themselves as unique. They encourage school performance and the use of libraries. They share ideas and assist, if needed, with homework. They treat children like intelligent beings who very often have good ideas and sound solutions to problems.

How to work is best taught by demonstration and involvement. Parents who show their children how to handle tools and machinery, without being too critical in the process, help the children develop confidence and self-esteem. Distribution of family chores (dependent upon the ages and capacities of the children and the family situation) teaches children that getting the daily work done can enhance life because it leads to order instead of disorder. Like play, work can be overemphasized. When it is, many people begin to think of it as distasteful. Later, they may choose boring jobs that require neither logical nor creative thinking. An effective parent, by example and precept, shows that work is often enjoyable—both the process of doing it and the product when it is done.

How to play is sometimes the most difficult thing for parents to teach, because they have structured their own lives without play. Thus they demonstrate, in their living and teaching, a "don't enjoy" injunction. Such parents do not know that play is the "work" of childhood. In play, children experiment with life roles. They use their imagination and expand their creativity. Playing with peers, they learn new interpersonal skills and the value of cooperation for achieving goals. So one of the most important parental tasks is encouraging children to play. People whose parents did not value play need a new Parent who does. Laughter often liberates by reducing personal or interpersonal tension. A playful person can laugh and love, think and work, with more enjoyment for life, liberty, and the pursuit of happiness.

Education in Feeling

It is impossible in this book to consider all the feelings or emotions that people have and how they can be recognized and dealt with. Yet, the new Parent is likely to need some guidance on the subject.

In one way or another, verbally or nonverbally, many children receive parental messages such as "Don't feel" or "Don't let your feelings show." Some children are encouraged to express their feelings, but others are not. They may be conditioned to be scared, yet not allowed to show it, with threats like "If you go on crying, I'll really give you something to cry about." Another way parents educate children about feelings is more subtle. They make statements such as "Big boys don't cry" or "Nice girls don't get angry." These messages need to be updated with statements such as "Boys can cry sometimes; it's natural" and "Girls do get angry sometimes, it's natural." All feelings are natural and need to be expressed and respected.

In response to being manipulated by parents, growing children learn to manipulate themselves and their feelings. In choosing whether to feel angry or sad, they may habitually choose how they felt in childhood. They may believe they have no choice except to be possessed by their negative feelings. However, feelings cannot possess anyone. Instead, people possess their feelings, and they have many choices about how to respond.

It is not unusual for children whose parent figures act hysterical or "crazy" to decide not to show *any* feelings. They may be afraid that they will go crazy if they let go. It is also common for people to block their tears, fearing that if they start crying, their tears will be seen as a mark of weakness or become a waterfall that never ends.

Many physical illnesses are created or made worse by negative feelings, by continuing stress, and by psychological problems. Psychotherapy may sometimes enhance a person's health and wellness. Some indications for psychotherapy are intense anxiety, with sweating and faintness; sleep disturbance; substance abuse, including excessive use of alcohol; a sense of impending disaster; suspiciousness or fatigue when there seems to be no cause; obsessiveness; destructiveness to self, others, or property; loss of memory; inappropriate behavior or speech; apathy or impaired functioning. These symptoms, experienced at a fairly low level of intensity, are fairly common. When the symptoms interfere with a sense of freedom and an active search for happiness, professional help is needed.

Mad, Sad, Scared, or Happy?

For convenience, feelings can be grouped into four basic categories: mad, sad, scared, and happy. Children use simple words to talk about how they feel. More sophisticated words come later when vocabulary increases and nuances surface. Within each category of feelings—mad, sad, scared, and happy—words reflect many levels of intensity. For example, when people say they are mad at someone, the feeling may be a frustration, which is a fairly low level of anger, or it may be rage, a much more intense level.

The value of expressing anger is often debated. When anger is released, more energy is available. Sometimes, getting angry is a healthy response to a serious threat and may even be lifesaving. Sometimes anger can be life-threatening as is the case on crowded freeways when road rage may cause someone to act unsafely or improperly.

Many professionals encourage the outward expression of anger because it becomes self-destructive when turned inward. Yelling, while pounding pillows, is a common therapeutic technique used to release hostile feelings.

Manipulation through anger is not uncommon. Persons who are easily angered often justify it on the grounds that it is effective. Like three-year-olds having temper tantrums to manipulate parents, they may get what they want in the short term. Most grown-ups eventually discover that this not an effective way to increase their long-term happiness.

Based on personal or cultural values, most people believe they are entitled to get angry about certain things and are self-righteous in doing so. Whether or not they have the right, excess anger is often accompanied by feelings of guilt or depression. The new Parent needs to recognize this and to set firm limits on the inner Child, so that rage is not expressed in destructive ways.

Sadness is another basic category and can also be related to cultural values. For example, in some cultures people laugh at bad luck, in others they swear, in still others they cry. Sadness includes feelings such as grief, loneliness, despair, and depression.

> *"When anger rises, think of the consequences."*
> —Confucius

Sadness is debilitating, and when people experience it deeply, they may withdraw physically or emotionally, thinking "I can't go on" or "I have nothing left to give" or "I don't want to live if it's going to be like this." Depression is the most widespread and serious form of sadness. Sometimes it has a biological or biochemical basis. Sometimes, it is due to a negative view of oneself or the world. Depression can be caused by a conflict of values or the inability to make a decision. Also, people who are afraid of the intensity of their anger may find it safer to block it out and feel depressed.

Substituting one feeling for another usually occurs without any conscious effort. In any event, the basic problem remains unsolved. Whatever the cause, depression represents a depth of sadness that is the opposite of happiness, just as despair is the opposite of hope.

Grief is another form of sadness. It occurs when people experience a major loss, and it is a natural response, especially after the loss of friends or family. In addition, the loss of some bodily function, a lifetime dream, a job, a home, a pet, or a prized possession often elicits sadness or grief.

When grieving, people experience physical symptoms of distress, such as headaches, insomnia, loss of appetite, or stomachaches. They may feel panic because of the inability to think. They may feel guilt, resentment, or hostility and be unable to accomplish routine tasks.

Like sadness and grief, feeling scared also has levels of intensity ranging from apprehension through anxiety, fear, terror, and panic. There is a natural apprehension before taking an exam or making an important speech or performing in some way that is subject to other people's judgment. Although some people are not apprehensive before these kinds of events, others experience anxiety or actual fear. Those who are most afraid may expect to be emotionally hurt or judged inadequate. They believe that criticism will somehow reduce their personal strength and lower their self-esteem.

Anxiety is a generalized feeling, perhaps overall nervousness, rather than an identifiable specific feeling like fear. Anxiety can be a response to the past, the present, or the future. It often produces physical symptoms like tics, headaches, or agitation. A person may feel anxious without knowing why. Negative fantasies increase the anxiety level and can be overpowering. The person suffering anxiety may be afraid of "falling apart." As a result, some people ridicule themselves or are ridiculed by others: "You dummy, there's nothing to be worried about."

Fear is more painful than anxiety. It is both more immediate and future-oriented. It occurs when there is an expectation that something very bad is going to happen. People with this expectation may also feel horror, loathing, dread, or panic.

Fear is a natural response to threatening situations. However, fear that was appropriate in the past is sometimes carried over into later life. When this occurs, people are fearful when there isn't anything to be afraid of. They may try to avoid any person or situation even remotely similar to what was feared in the past. If the fear becomes very intense, a person may experience overwhelming terror, collapse physically or emotionally, and become unable to cope with daily tasks or decide on long-range goals.

People who are frequently fearful, yet able to control it somewhat, go through life procrastinating to avoid making wrong choices. They may get mad at themselves or be sad for not being different. A potent new Parent is needed to protect the scared person (who might need to uncover and confront the original sources of fear).

Everyone wants to feel happy more often and for longer periods of time. Happiness has levels of intensity, just as the other basic feelings do. Satisfaction, contentment, and pleasure are at one level. Delight, elation, bliss, and ecstasy are at higher levels of intensity.

One of the characteristics of intense happiness is that it does not last. It either becomes less intense (though still pleasurable) or is negatively transformed. The transformation can be due to changes in the external situation, such as waking up happy then going to work and being fired. On the other hand, changes may be due to internal dynamics, such as being ill or even feeling guilty for being happy. It is the job of the new Parent to clear away the negative attitudes that prevent us from having more and more happiness in our lives.

Tough Love/Tender Love

Each of us needs an internalized Parent who supports us in being and doing. Learning how to balance being and doing requires skill. Like a gymnast who knows the value of balance, a person in the process of self-parenting needs a new Parent who will encourage both.

Unless both being and doing are encouraged and developed, happiness is always an elusive butterfly, just out of reach.

Sometimes, in childhood, *being* is stressed by adoring, overly nurturing parents. As a result, their children often feel entitled to everything they desire and are not motivated to establish goals that call for personal initiative or effort. They want what they want when they want it. They may become so self-centered that they need a new Parent who will use tough love.

People who have been overindulged typically act on impulse and may be inconsistent or unreliable. They often undermine their own success by doing such things as speaking without thinking, acting without planning, or spending money without budgeting. They want to do what they want without regard for other people, want love without acting lovable, want happiness without commitment, want freedom without responsibility. These people need firm a new Parent who will help them regulate their behavior.

The opposite type of person needs a tender new Parent. This is often true of those who have had brutal, overly strict, or highly critical parents who demanded perfect performance. These people need affirmation for *being* alive and being who they are, not just recognition for *doing* chores or school tasks.

> *"A friend is a gift you give yourself."*
> —*Robert Louis Stevenson*

Many people imagine they need tender, encouraging love when they may actually need tough love. You need tender, encouraging love if you were not affirmed for being you and if you frequently experience a sense of despair or depression. You need firm, perhaps tough, love if your capacities for achievement, for independent thinking, and for action were not encouraged, if you act passive instead of assertive, or if you procrastinate often. When people identify whether they need tender or tough love, they take charge of their lives and take responsibility for their own happiness.

Learning Something New

The parent figures in your childhood may not have encouraged you to learn from a position of self-confidence. They may have given you the message that learning is tough work and that learning something new will always be a struggle. That may be true for learning how computer programs work, but it is not necessarily true in reprogramming yourself.

Granted, learning something new may be a challenge,

even difficult. It's hard to change habits such as coaching yourself to be outgoing if you've been shy all your life. But too often, we focus only on the first steps to learning something new, and those first steps are often the hardest.

Look at a total whole life experience, and you'll see that learning difficult things does not have to be agonizing or frustrating. It can be pleasurable. When you see progress, you'll feel both relief and satisfaction, which is often followed by continued progress and increased happiness.

Use the thinking, data processing, and analytical capacities of your Adult ego state to continue educating your new Parent. Then your new Parent will be able to take good care of you. It won't be long before you can look beyond those difficult first steps to important signs of success and happiness. Try it, you'll like it.

Discovery Tools

Parenting and the Three Ps

Consider areas in your life in which you experienced your parent figures being potent, such as protecting you, and giving you permission—especially permission to be happy. Describe specific situations in which the following occurred.

- When my parents were potent:
  The effect on me was:
- When my parents were not potent:
  The effect on me was:
- When my parents gave me protection:

The effect on me was:
- When my parents did not give me protection:
  The effect on me was:
- When my parents gave me permission:
  The effect on me was:
- When my parents did not give me permission:
  The effect on me was:

If your past parental figures were not potent enough to give you the permission and protection you needed, what do you need to add—beginning now—to your new Parent ego state?

Write your answer in your notebook or journal.

- My new Parent needs to:
- The effect of this on me would be:

The Three Ps in Problem Solving

Remember that your teachers were like parent substitutes and your parents were like teacher substitutes. They all taught you a great deal—some good, some bad.

Think of an unsolved problem you currently have.

- In what ways do you need a potent parent-mentor-coach to help you?
- What protective strategies are needed for solving the problem?
- What permissions would be useful?
- Is your life, your liberty, or your pursuit of happiness part of this problem?

• Is someone else's life, liberty, or pursuit of happiness part of this problem?

• Keep in mind that parents are teachers and teachers are parents, so get involved with the reeducation of your inner Child.

Learning the Easy and Hard Ways

People learn in many ways. Sometimes the learning comes the hard way, with struggle, anxiety, or agony. For example, some people only learn out of fear of punishment or after making a costly mistake.

Sometimes learning comes the easy way, without struggle and with interest and enjoyment.

• In your notebook or journal, list five important things you have learned and mark each one for how you learned it, the easy way or the hard way.

• Explain the effect you feel each new learned thing had on you.

Now sit down and relax your body, especially your shoulders and facial muscles. Imagine you are in a situation where you need to learn something new and difficult. If you are anxious or confused, see yourself appearing confident and relaxed.

Say to yourself, "I am able to learn many things the easy way." Repeat this several times until you really believe it.

Select something you want to learn now. Say to yourself, "I can learn (fill in the blank) the easy way."

Basic Education for Living

The basic educational task for parents is helping children learn how to love, think, work, and play. Consider how you learned each of these in childhood from your parents or parent figures. Also think about whether you are satisfied or dissatisfied with what you learned and how you learned it.

- How I learned to love:
  Satisfied or dissatisfied?
- How I learned to think:
  Satisfied or dissatisfied?
- How I learned to work:
  Satisfied or dissatisfied?
- How I learned to play:
  Satisfied or dissatisfied?

If you are dissatisfied with what you learned and/or how you learned it, then you need some reeducation.

Design one to three short statements for any area of basic education that you missed. In your notebook or journal, write statements your new Parent could use. (These can be very specific—"You can learn to think clearly about mathematics—" or more generalized—"You don't need to be confused.")

Now, put the statements on 3x5 cards and carry them with you. Read them several times a day.

Recognizing Feelings

Following is a list of feelings many people experience. Note the ones that apply to you, think about how often you feel them, and consider how the feelings affect your behavior. Also, ask yourself how others respond to you when you're experiencing any one of these feelings.

Sad
Grieved
Angry
Ashamed
Guilty
Confused
Inadequate
Jealous
Bored
Anxious
Scared
Relaxed
Lively
Loving
Excited
Sexy
Confident
Free
Happy

Have some of these unpleasant feelings become so frequent that they are similar to habits that you want to change and don't know how?

What do you need to add to your developing new Parent to create more understanding about your feelings?

Redecisions and the New Parent

As you get acquainted with some of your childhood

patterns about feeling and not feeling, begin to consider whether you need to make some redecisions.

Sit quietly. Take a few deep breaths and let your body and face relax. Release tension from your muscles. Loosen your jaw and lips, relax the muscles around your eyes, and let your breathing become slower.

Imagine there is a TV screen in front of you and the story of your life is being played.

Look closely at scenes where you are showing a lot of emotion.

Then look at scenes where you are not showing the emotions you are actually feeling. Perhaps you are afraid to show how you feel or believe it won't do any good.

Now look at any scenes that typically call for some emotional response, to which you are not responding either internally or externally.

As you consider the kinds of scenes you identified above, do you think your new Parent needs to be more tender in encouraging you to really feel? Or do you need a firmer Parent, who will encourage you to experience your feelings in healthy, nonexploitative ways?

Educating the Parent to Tenderness

Many people need to reparent themselves with a tender Parent who will encourage success, forgive failures, and encourage relaxation and play. Do you need a tender Parent? Decide if you seldom, occasionally, or frequently experience each of the symptoms below.

- Can't think under stress
- Panic if making a mistake

- Depressed if not perfect
- Scared of disapproval
- Workaholic
- Don't know how to play
- Basically afraid
- Basically anxious

If you decided "frequently" more than any other category, you may need a tender Parent.

If so, what steps can you take to begin?

What might this new, tender Parent say to you that would be effective in alleviating the negative symptom or symptoms?

The Need for Limits

Many people need to reparent themselves with a firm Parent who will not allow them to behave impulsively and eat, drink, or spend money when it is not in their best interests. To find out if you would benefit from a firm Parent who will encourage you to set limits, consider the list below and decide how often each one applies to you: seldom, occasionally, or frequently.

- Explode angrily
- Get hysterical
- Fall into depression
- Eat or drink too much
- Smoke when I know I shouldn't
- Avoid exercising
- Make promises I don't keep
- Spend money I can't afford

- Give advice without thinking
- Act helpless when I'm not
- Act self-indulgent
- Act impulsive

If you decided "frequently" in several categories, you probably need a firm Parent in those areas of your life, one who can coach you to set limits and use more self-control.

If you agree, how can you begin to reeducate yourself to set limits?

What might your new, firm Parent say to you that would be effective in helping you to set limits?

What reward would you deem appropriate for succeeding?

Midpoint Evaluation

Synectic is a word that refers to the novel joining together of elements that are not readily seen as connected. In developing your new Parent, you are using synectic skills because you are using both logic and creativity. This is approximately a midway point in your self-reparenting and a good place to evaluate your progress. On a sheet of your notebook or journal:

- Summarize how you have used your logical thinking so far in self-reparenting.
- Summarize how you have used your creative thinking so far in self-reparenting.
- Put the two together and evaluate how you are doing in your pursuit of happiness.

5

Listening to Yourself with Love

Have you ever said to yourself or to someone else, "I wish I knew what I really want"?

Or have you ever said to yourself "I'll never get what I need. Nobody cares. I might as well give up"?

Do you ever wonder how your life would be different if you could just find inner peace instead of turmoil?

Do you ever feel as if you're not put together in the right way, and you don't know what the right way is?

If so, it's time to discover more about what the child part of you needed and wanted when you were a child. Knowing that will give you more freedom to be who you want to be and to do what you want to do. It will give you more freedom to get on with your life.

The ability of any child to be creative, spontaneous, autonomous, and also able to feel close to others is usually directly affected by childhood authorities who have the power to create what feels like either a prison or an open healthy world.

A Look Ahead

It's hard to be happy until you have freed yourself from

some of the pain of the past. Yet, it's never too late to start this process. You begin by discovering how you shaped your needs and wants to please authority figures; how you learned to comply, rebel, or procrastinate around authorities; and how you may still do the same—at least sometimes—in your current life.

In this chapter, you will learn how to enter into dialogue with your inner Child. This inner part of your personality has much to tell you about specific needs and wants. With this knowledge, you can learn to function as a liberating parent, an encouraging coach, and a knowledgeable mentor. Each role can help in your pursuit of happiness.

Born to Love

Everyone hopes to be loved, and this hope, for many people, is realized. Love is life-giving: it heals, it liberates, and, in its best forms, it is intense, durable, and unconditional. Genuine love makes us capable of sacrifice when sacrifice is needed and is offered without exploitation. It is goodwill freely given, asking nothing in return.

Attachment is not the same as love. People are often legally or emotionally attached to others they do not even like or respect. It is a tragedy when there is no love between parents and their children. Children are born to love and be loved.

Unfortunately, for a variety of reasons, parents may treat their children so that the children do not feel lovable or loving. Disliking and even hating themselves, these children can get into patterns of self-destructiveness or lash out to inflict damage on objects or pets or people. Those who experience too much physical or emotional pain do not believe in the miracle of love. They need to be healed with the kind of love that gives them protection and permission. If this healing succeeds, it can release, at any time during their lives, their capacity to be loving and allow them to claim the birthright of being loved.

Parents who expect appreciation or high performance from children as payment for "loving" them pollute the relationship, much as clear water can be polluted. The new internal Parent must be able to love without exploiting the inner Child.

How Needs and Wants Are Adapted

Children adapt their needs and wants to parents, parent figures, and their environment in many ways. They may obey like "good" little boys or girls, argue and fight back, or use delaying techniques if asked to help.

These adaptations fall into three basic categories: compliance, rebellion, and procrastination. Being compliant is usually based on the belief that obedience will bring love, or will at least decrease the chance of being punished. Being rebellious often happens because a child does not consider the parents' demands loving or rational. Procrastination is a wavering between the two: "Perhaps my parents will love me (or forgive me) if I eventually do what they want."

Although everyone uses all these responses from time to time, a continuing pattern of procrastination and rebellion can become a major problem, both in childhood and in later life. Some parents punish children for this behavior.

Others deal with it from a caring perspective, setting reasonable limits and reasonable consequences. Still other parents ignore rebelliousness and thus may encourage it—intentionally or not—and a child can become a tyrant. Tyrants are hard to love. They want total liberty for themselves and total obedience from others.

Many parents believe that one of their primary tasks is training their children to comply. The training may be indiscriminate and thus destroy a child's sense of self-esteem. It may also be reasonable and increase a child's sense of self-esteem. It may fluctuate at different times, for different reasons, around different subjects.

Parents teaching compliance usually justify their actions; they are "only doing their duty." But all too often they interpret their duty as the need to develop obedient children—in other words, "good" children, who will not talk back, will not think independently, and who will not rebel against parental dictates.

Children who are taught compliance obey without thinking and have little capacity to make independent decisions in later life. As adults, these people are easily swayed by others, are reluctant to take risks, and seldom question the system. They follow orders, even when the results may be bad for someone else or themselves.

Rebellion against authority often shows itself in early childhood if children feel unappreciated or unloved. First comes a sense of being treated unfairly. Next comes the decision "I won't do what they want" or "I'll get even for what they did to me." The needs and wants of children are often just the opposite of those of their parents.

"I want you to pick up your toys," the parent might say.

"I won't!" a child may respond. "Don't you dare talk to me like that!" may come next. The child's rebellion may then escalate outwardly into a temper tantrum or be sublimated and built up internally as defiance.

Defiance is an attitude sometimes expressed in bold or insolent ways, sometimes in soft and procrastinating ways. Regardless of the mask it wears, defiance is an attempt to be free from authoritarian demands.

> *"Power abdicates only under the stress of counter-power."*
> —*Martin Buber*

Parent figures, whether they are biological relatives, teachers in classrooms, private mentors, or organizational coaches, respond differently to defiance. Some call it "stubbornness" and try to manipulate the stubborn child into obedience. Others may call it "guts," complimenting the child who takes that "try and make me" stance. Still other parents feel powerless and throw up their hands in dismay. In so doing, they lose their ability to be adequate models and to influence their children effectively. They may love their children, but they don't know how to show it.

Rebellious children usually continue acting defiant in later life, even without cause. They are difficult to be with, since, when they don't get their way, they throw adult versions of their childhood temper tantrums. They are difficult to reach emotionally; their defiance acts as a barrier to love and intimacy.

Procrastination is what some children use against authorities when they want to rebel and don't want to comply. In procrastinating, they are trying to come to some kind of workable compromise that satisfies the inner war. Procrastination is a compromise, and "Just a minute" or "I'll do it later" is usually a safer way to ignore authorities and protect a sense of independence than directly saying "No." Parents' demanding or authoritative behavior toward their children often fosters procrastination.

Procrastination is usually a slightly hidden form of rebellion. Children with demanding parents who frequently order "Do this" or "Do that" may adapt by developing delaying techniques. Repressive parents who often say "Don't talk back" or "Don't ask so many questions" or "Shut up" may force their children to be quiet, go slow, and not ask for much. Such children need new messages of encouragement so that they can learn to act positively and with alacrity.

Sometimes procrastination can be a sign of a child who has not yet learned how to make decisions and is afraid of making a wrong one. Occasionally, procrastination is used to manipulate others into taking on responsibility for the procrastinator or the procrastinator's assigned tasks. It is not unusual for the procrastinator to withdraw from loving relationships with others.

We are all familiar with the procrastinating adult! Who of us has not put off some unpleasant task? But serious procrastinators can be deeply troubled, and all procrastination usually has a hidden agenda. Immobilized by fear or acting out of repressed rebellion, the procrastinator appears to be trying, but is actually sabotaging his or her own life.

"Nobody Loves Me"

When people rebel, procrastinate, or withdraw, it is often because they believe they are not lovable. When constantly criticized or told "no," this reinforces their belief. They may try to be perfect or to manipulate others to comply with their demands and, if not successful, feel frustrated and (sometimes) erupt into violence.

When these inner childhood beliefs continue into adult life, change is needed. The person who complies a lot needs new parental messages such as "You can think well for yourself," "You can decide what's right for you," or "Set your own time schedule if you want to."

The person who is overly rebellious needs new parental messages like "You can get what you want in better ways," "You don't have to have such a hot temper," and "Don't get so uptight about little things."

The person who procrastinates too often also needs new parental messages like "Don't take so long to make up your mind. Decide now and then go for it," "You don't have to make perfect decisions," and "If something goes wrong, you have the ability to straighten it out."

It can be helpful to write your new messages on 3x5 cards and put them in strategic places—on the bathroom mirror, the refrigerator door, or on your desk at work where you'll see them often. These new messages can be interpreted as coming from the healthy new Parent, coach, or mentor you are designing for yourself.

The Importance of Touch

The earliest adaptations that result in compliance, rebellion, and procrastination are partly related to the way children are touched when they are young. In severe cases parents beat their children, sexually molest them, or deny them food or other necessities to get them to obey. This may lead to external compliance, to rebellion (as when a child runs away), or to generalized insolence, generated by rage that is held back temporarily. This rage may later be expressed as brutality toward people or pets who are weaker. It may also be expressed hurtfully toward oneself. Hating or hurting one's body—or an insatiable craving to be touched—often has its beginnings in unhealthy touch or lack of touch in childhood. Even in "normal" families, many parents have a hard time expressing their love with physical gestures or loving behavior.

If lovingly cared for, children will respond with love. The responsive smiles and wiggles of infants show that humans are equipped at birth for healthy relationships and intimacy. Frequent touching, rocking, carrying, and holding all stimulate an infant's well-being. Without sufficient touching, infants become sick, even die. For maximum mental and physical health, healthy loving touch is an absolute necessity. This is just as true when you become an adult. As you begin to know the needs and wants of your inner Child, you may discover fear of some kinds of touch and longing for other kinds.

The importance of touch begins at birth. The first gasp for breath, the shock of cooler air, and bright lights can be made easier by the caressing of human hands. Liberation from the protective womb, into a world that is not always protective, is an event of great magnitude. Infants who are not separated from their mothers immediately seem to have a greater sense of trust about the world around them.

Contact comfort with softness and warmth is the most

important variable in the famous Harlow studies of monkey behavior. The studies show that laboratory monkeys separated from their own mothers at birth selected soft cloth mother-surrogates for contact comfort, even though a wire-mesh surrogate could feed them. In like manner, infants cling to the softness of their mothers and, if they are not available, are often happy with a soft blanket or toy.

> *"Memory is a diary that we all carry with us."*
> —*Oscar Wilde*

Later in life, softness in another person is certainly preferred to harshness. Interestingly enough, when people increase the amount of soft and loving touch they give and receive, their faces often soften, and frequently they look years younger.

Sometimes I Feel Like a Motherless Child

Being physically or emotionally forced into compliance is an intrusion that interferes with the growth of self-esteem. Without self-esteem and the permissions and protections that encourage it, some children feel they have no parents—that they have been abandoned. It's impossible, then, to feel happy.

Being abandoned by a parent leaves a terrible scar, and feeling like a motherless or fatherless child may be reexperienced in adulthood when things go wrong. Whatever the inadequacies of the parents who are present, there is still a yearning to believe that some things about the parents were positive and that their inadequacies were due to circumstances in their own childhood over which they had no control.

All of us need to be comforted when things go wrong. If our parents are missing or other family members and friends do not act in caring ways, the feeling of being motherless or fatherless can be overwhelming. The old spiritual "Sometimes I feel like a motherless child a long way from home" touches the wellsprings of many who hunger or thirst for what they missed.

Listening to Self-Talk

The main reason so many people feel motherless or fatherless is that their parents were absent by reason of death, desertion, divorce, or disinterest. The most common way disinterest is expressed is in not listening. Children need and want to be heard. Many people feel that they were not listened to enough when they were little or, if listened to, were not understood.

One of the skills important to self-reparenting is listening to your own inner Child. Children who are not really listened to may give up trying to be heard, withdraw, and become loners. Or they may become depressed and mumble, as if what they have to say isn't important. In contrast, some children who do not get listened to decide to act in rebellious or aggressive ways. Desperate for attention, they may do almost anything to get it.

People tend to have conversations going on inside their heads so constantly that they may not be aware of them. Sometimes they hear a parental reprimand for not having said or done certain things "correctly." Sometimes what they hear is parental encouragement. Sometimes it is a lament of the Child, or a repetition of a childhood decision such as

"I really hate him, and I'm going to get even" or "I'm so scared I'm going to run away" or "I can't stand being alone; I feel like I'm going crazy" or "I'll never make it. I'll never be good enough." Learning to listen to this inner talking is an important part of reparenting yourself.

Learning how to listen to self-talk has many advantages. Listening to your own internal Parent-Child arguments may clarify inner conflicts, ambiguities, or incongruities. Learning

> "It takes two to speak the truth—one to speak and the other to hear."
> —Henry Thoreau

how to listen to your inner Child's defensive statements and excuses can reveal unmet needs and wants, just as learning how to listen to one's body and its SOS signals for more rest or exercise, more food or less, more loving care and less neglect can actually be lifesaving.

When There Are No Words

Everyone was once an infant and may occasionally respond to life experiences totally at the feeling level—nonverbally, with cries, screams, or gurgles of delight.

Such regression can occur during times of stress or crisis, when a person may feel helpless, unable to think or even talk. Reliving traumatic childhood experiences, perhaps in trance or hypnotic states, may also induce regression. At such times the person may feel totally incapacitated and unable to take appropriate action. The Child who has no words needs an inner Parent who is encouraging and supportive instead of critical or sadistic.

During the time the new Parent is being constructed, the rational, clear-thinking Adult part of the personality must be in charge. The new Parent under construction is unable to provide enough protection and support. The logical thought, analysis of a situation, and a safe resolution of difficulties must be provided by the Adult ego state in order to protect the Child. It must not seem to be deserting or abandoning the Child. The inner Child will know if that occurs and will return to its previous unhappy state.

To avoid this, a person's Adult needs to be in continuing contact with the Child, offering logical and sane resolution methods to challenging situations that may arise. Sometimes it helps people to hold a pillow in their arms and rock back and forth. This is an aid to the Child, who begins to experience (or reexperience) much-needed nurturing and the support of a loving new Parent.

When Dialogue is Only Monologue

Dialogue is the open give and take of information, ideas, and even dreams. When people are truly in dialogue, they understand each other. However, much talk that goes on between people is monologue disguised as dialogue. Those involved are so preoccupied with what they want to say that they do not really listen to each other.

Monologic conversation is expressed in four ways: when thoughts are pointedly expressed without consideration for the other person, when each talks without purpose except to make some kind of impression, when each considers his own opinions to be right and the other person's opinions to be doubtful, when each talks about his own experiences without caring about the other.

In monologue, people talk past each other instead of to each other. Instead of actually listening, they are planning what they are going to say when the other person stops talking or they are planning how to avoid another encounter.

In contrast, people who are in a genuine dialogic relationship with each other have a sense of "we." This may be temporary or continuing. When it exists, each feels open to the other and honestly connected. This is ideal for a parent-child relationship and inner Parent to inner Child con-

> "The most called-upon prerequisite of a friend is an accessible ear."
> —Maya Angelou

versation. Each is truly willing to listen to the other and share information as well as hopes and dreams. It also is an achievable ideal for an inner Parent and inner Child relationship. In the process of self-reparenting a new Parent can be created with the genuine dialogic ability to listen with love.

Needs and Wants Are Not the Same

Freedom to experience the creative and happy Child within depends on whether that Child's needs and wants are lovingly heard. Survival depends on having basic physical needs met. People experience these needs as absolute: "I'm so thirsty I can't stand it" or "I'm so cold I feel as though I'm freezing to death" or "I'm so tired I feel like collapsing." Physical needs can often be satisfied by some object or action: a drink, a sweater, a nap, or food.

Wants are different. Getting what you want is seldom necessary for survival, yet is often desired to improve the quality of life. To want is to wish to have something that is missing or to have more of something. The wanting of the inner Child can be intense, especially for those who experience emotional deprivation. For them, it may actually become a survival need.

The words *want* and *need* are often used interchangeably. "I really *need* to go out to dinner tonight" may in fact be "I *want* to go out to dinner tonight because I don't want to cook." "I *want* to go to bed early" may instead be "My body really *needs* rest."

The energy people put into pleasing themselves and getting what they want may be more or less than they use to satisfy their needs. In affluent, consumer-oriented societies, some people may be so self-satisfied that they do not distinguish between their wants and needs.

When people give up hope, they cease to want. Instead of wanting something to be different and being motivated to do something about it, they begin to daydream, or they give up their dreams and resign themselves to unhappiness.

People who do not like themselves, or who imagine no one else could like them, may deny their own wants or ignore their own needs. Those who do not like or respect other people will also believe that others do not have the right to get their needs or wants met.

Getting our needs met is essential and getting our wants met is important. Happiness increases when these occur.

Love Is Action

People can endure almost any catastrophe if they know they are lovable and if they are able to show love to others.

Love is not just warm feelings; love is action. Parents who love a child intensely take care of its body, mind, and spirit and encourage the child to treat them with respect. Good parents love so deeply that they willingly sacrifice time and energy because of love. To parents who believe that love is action, not just warm feelings, caring for their children is not resented but is always a high priority. Thus, when the child has an important need or want, the loving parent rearranges priorities to deal with it. This is especially important when the child is young and requires intense involvement.

> *"Action is eloquence."*
> *—Shakespeare*

Later in life, the one-to-one intensity needs to be transformed so that the child can learn to love more extensively. Many people talk of loving everything and everybody, yet they may not show it. Others only love themselves and one or two others. Between the extremes can be a healthy balance. In self-reparenting, a new Parent needs to know that every person is important—that love is not a scarce commodity, and there is enough love to go around.

Love in action may be brief, as when someone briefly risks his or her own life for another and doesn't wait for thanks. Or, love may be a lifelong relationship, as in some marriages or friendships. Good parents make this permanent commitment to their children as persons, even though they may not agree with some of their values or lifestyles. In self-reparenting, a person's new Parent must have a similar orientation, which is to stay active, never to desert the inner Child, and always to show love—no matter what.

Adequacy of parental love can be measured in two ways: loving involvement and parenting skills. Some parents who love their children and are emotionally involved with them do not have adequate parenting skills. For example, they may be overly indulgent of inappropriate behavior or overly indulgent by trying to give their children "everything." As a result, their children often become spoiled, act irresponsibly with possessions, or manipulate others dishonestly to get more. Most of this behavior occurs because the parents are inadequate in parenting skills and unwise in gift-giving.

Another inadequacy in parental care occurs when parents do *not* love their children and are emotionally distant, even though they may have parenting skills. They do not enjoy the positive emotional involvement with their children that comes about while learning and working, playing and loving together. They do their parenting out of a sense of duty, or so they will look good in the eyes of the neighbors.

Whether parents are loving and uninformed, or informed and unloving, the result is similar because the parenting is inadequate. In developing your new Parent, you will need to decide to love your inner Child just because the Child is important and to love this Child to a degree such that the Child becomes free to love others. Your own Child needs to be loved permanently and unconditionally, regardless of mistakes and imperfections. And, your inner Child needs the wisdom of loving concern combined with firmness. When people are loved, they can learn to love themselves and the rest of the world and experience liberty and happiness at the deepest levels. They can become friends with the universe.

The root of the word *friend* means "free"—not in bondage. The Old English word *freon* means to love, and the word *freond* becomes the modern English word friend. In the process of self-reparenting, the new Parent does not hold the Child in bondage. Instead, the Parent respects the nobility and the mobility of the Child and rejoices over its emerging independence. The two of them become friends.

Listen with Love

Love can be compared with water. Everybody needs it and wants it. Like an ocean, love can have depth. Like a storm at sea, it can have intensity. Like a still pond in a meadow, it can be quiet. Like a quickly moving mountain stream, it can be pure. Like the power from a waterfall, it can energize. Love not only quenches thirst, but it can also wash clean.

The continuing task of your self-reparenting process is to build a new Parent ego state that will listen to your inner Child lovingly. It must ask the Child in you, time and time again, "What do you need? What do you want?" Then, listening with love, the new Parent will accept some overcompliance, rebellion, procrastination, and withdrawal and will encouragingly remind your inner Child of your action-based program for happiness.

> *"I do not love him because he is good, but because he is my little child."*
> —Rabindranath Tagore

Discovery Tools

Your Response to Authority Then

Make a list of demands made on you in childhood, with your typical response to each of these demands; how you complied, rebelled, or procrastinated.

- Childhood demands:
  How I complied:
  How I rebelled:
  How I procrastinated:

How was your response to some authorities different from your response to others? Why do you suppose that was?

Your Response to Authority Now

Make a list of demands currently being made on you by yourself or by others (spouse, parents, children, boss) and how you tend to respond.

- Current demands
  How I rebel:
  How I comply:
  How I procrastinate:

How is your response to some authorities different from your response to others? What do you think is the reason for this? Is your response pattern similar to that of your childhood?

What advice might a wise, loving new Parent give you? Would you rebel or procrastinate against the advice, or would you accept it? If you would rebel or procrastinate, how might the new Parent rephrase the advice to make it acceptable?

Your Touch Portrait

This exercise is designed to help you discover how and where you like to be touched or don't like to be touched as it relates to your childhood.

Draw two full-length portraits of yourself. Make one a front view and one a back view.

Draw little whirls or circles on the parts of you that were lovingly touched in childhood.

Leave blank those parts of you that were seldom or never touched in childhood.

Make crisscross lines where you were touched in embarrassing or hurtful ways.

As you consider your touch portraits, what are the implications for your life now? What does your inner Child need relative to this touch portrait from a healthy new Parent?

Current Touch Preferences

As you think of your childhood and how you were touched, consider your preferences in your current life.

Many families and other cultural groups have customs about how physically close people should be, including how to shake hands, how to kiss, hug, or have sex, how to touch or not touch children and so forth.

What are some of the cultural beliefs and patterns you have about touch and how did you develop them?

• Touching I like or am comfortable with:
    How I learned this:
• Touching I dislike or am uncomfortable with:
    How I learned this:

Is there anything you want to change about what you currently like or dislike about touching? If so, what can you begin to do to facilitate this?

Music to Remember

Have you ever found yourself humming a song over and over and suddenly realized that what you were humming reflected an unsolved problem? Maybe the purpose of the song was to give you the courage to take action or to move you from depression to hope or to remind you that you are lovable.

In similar ways, the music you heard when you were growing up may have influenced you.

• What were some of the lullabies or other songs you heard frequently when you were a child?
• Did you ever feel like a motherless child and have a favorite song or lullaby that reflected that feeling?
• What were some songs that were most popular during your high school years? When you were a young adult?
• Were the songs romantic? Nostalgic? Stirring? Pious? Fun? Tearful? Patriotic? Inspirational? Liberating or enslaving?

What might you learn from your awareness of the music you remember?

Being Listened to

Let your memories drift back to your childhood and to various situations when you wanted to say something and you wanted people to listen to you. Note responses to the following in your journal or notebook.

- Situations when I wanted to say something and wanted to be listened to:
  - Responses from parent figures and others:
  - What I said to myself then:

Now consider your current life and whether people listen to you.

- Situations when I want to say something and be listened to:
  - Responses from parent figures and others:
  - What I usually say to myself:

Is there any similarity between the way people listen to you now and the way they did when you were young? Do you like it? If not, what can you change?

Confronting Unnecessary Fear

When people decide to ask others for what they need and want, or when they decide to go after it themselves, they often hold back because of fear. Fear of disapproval and punishment or fear of abandonment are the most common holdovers from childhood.

Some people fear success as well as failure. Still others are afraid of finding out who they really are under the skin.

This exercise is to help you clarify if you have unnecessary fears that interrupt your pursuit of happiness. Make three lists using the following prompts.

• Needs and wants I have that I don't pursue:

• Catastrophic or unreasonable expectations that hold me back:

• How a potent new Parent could help me eliminate or reduce fears:

Yes, You Can!

Sometimes you may feel that you won't be able to stick with your plans in a crisis. Yet, intellectually you know that you can. You know this because in the past you have often solved problems and are currently solving some problems. You are also thinking of potential problems and making plans for the future. So, you are already a problem solver.

In this exercise, write yourself a letter in three parts. Spend time on it. It is important.

• In part one, compliment yourself for problems you solved in the past by thinking them through.

• In part two of your letter, compliment yourself for the thinking you are doing now in your current life. Be specific about your compliments.

• In part three, compliment yourself for being able to predict that you will be able to think even better in the future.

Now file your letter some place where you will be able to find it easily in a crisis.

What Do You Want? What Do You Need?

This is one of the most important exercises in the entire process of self-reparenting. It will be a dialogue to discover what your Child needs and wants.

First, find a quiet place and get into a comfortable position. Let your eyelids drop; let your body go limp. Imagine you are in a pleasant setting, such as a lovely garden with flowers blooming and birds twittering or at the seashore where the sun is pleasant and the surf is quiet or in the mountains where the air is fresh and the sounds and smells are natural.

Speak internally to yourself as a child, using a loving, supportive voice and manner. Use an endearing term or affectionate name, as a parent might with a child, and ask yourself:

- "Is there anything you need now?"
- "What do you want now?"

Continue to use the two questions several times and listen for your inner Child to answer. Encourage a genuine inner dialogue.

Withhold all judgment at this time on whether what you want and need is good for you. Remember, good parents listen well.

List your Child's wants and needs. Don't evaluate; just list them.

- My Child needs:
- My Child wants:

Now consider how your ideal Parent could respond to these needs and wants.

Lovable? Who, Me?

Sit back, relax your shoulders, and reexperience the ways you were loved in childhood by your parents or parent substitutes, then write out the following.

- Times I knew I was loved:
- Times I doubted I was loved:
- How the love and nonlove were shown:
- Ways I could love myself more now:

Discovering Your Powers

Do you ever catch yourself thinking that happiness is just around the corner because a particular person will be showing up on your doorstep soon?

Do you ever dream of accumulating more and more and imagine it will bring you to an open door of power?

Do you ever struggle for recognition, believing that if you get recognition from others it will prove you are a valuable person?

Do you ever feel excited when you think of ways you are free to relax or play or try out a new hobby?

If so, you know the enjoyment of pursuit. You like setting goals. You pursue them with a sense of hope. You expect your achievements to bring you happiness and sometimes they do. However, at other times when you achieve your goals, you may find that your priorities have changed in some way and your new achievements seem irrelevant. They fail to bring the happiness you anticipated, and you may ask yourself: "What was it all about?" "Why did I waste my time and energy on something that doesn't really matter now?"

A Look Ahead

In this chapter you will discover that you have within you the power to be happy. You will learn more about your natural human needs for power, how these needs and desires may have been thwarted at one time, and how they can now be realized. For example, you will learn more about how hopefulness depends upon the ability to trust and how wisdom can develop when your acceptance of yourself and others expands.

This process of discovering your powers will start with a reconsideration of the pursuit of happiness that was once considered to be a human right.

Happiness by Legislation

The Declaration of Independence of the United States of America proclaimed that there were "certain unalienable rights, that among these are life, liberty and the pursuit of happiness." It goes on to say that the principles and powers of a government should be derived from the consent of the people and should be in a form most likely to effect safety and happiness. However, happiness was not legislated.

In 1787, the Constitution of the United States of America was signed. Although based on the philosophy of the Declaration of Independence, the right to pursue happiness was not included. Probably because happiness was interpreted as an internal experience that cannot be measured as can life and liberty.

In September of that same year, the first ten Amendments to the Constitution were passed by Congress. They were ratified in 1791 by three-fourths of the states. Commonly called the Bill of Rights, the right to pursue happiness was also omitted from the Amendments. In spite of that, the idea and words have become a national treasure.

> *"Happiness makes up in height for what it lacks in length."*
> *—Robert Frost*

In 1948, the General Assembly of the United Nations adopted the Universal Declaration of Human Rights as a standard for all people and nations. This document affirmed that equal and inalienable rights for all people are essential to freedom, justice, and peace and that international order is necessary for these rights and freedoms to be realized.

Personal happiness is not always an outcome from experiencing freedom, justice, and peace. Yet, the process of pursuing these things has such great appeal that people often achieve happiness when they engage in their pursuit.

Steps to Personal Power

Although there are many developmental theories regarding personality, there is no general agreement. Most theories have not taken sexual and cultural differences into account. However, Erik Erickson's developmental theory is widely used, and, although his research was male-oriented, it is useful as a general guide.

His concept is that particular human "virtues" develop at specific age levels for individuals who solve the basic crisis associated with that age. These virtues are the powers of hope, will, purpose, competence, fidelity, love, care, and wisdom.

People who possess these powers have overcome basic developmental challenges that come at specific ages. The ages, challenges, and positive results if the challenges are met successfully are as follows:

Age of Development	Developmental Crisis	Result if Crisis Is Solved
0–1½	Basic trust vs. mistrust	Hope
1½–3	Autonomy vs. shame and doubt	Will
3–7	Initiative vs. guilt	Purpose
7–12	Mastery vs. inferiority	Competence
12–18	Identity vs. identity confusion	Fidelity
18–30	Intimacy vs. isolation	Love
30–60	Generativity vs. stagnation	Care
Over 60	Ego integrity vs. despair	Wisdom

Later in his own life, Erickson concluded that in spite of the fact that individuals do not solve all their developmental issues, they nevertheless can and do sometimes leap ahead toward wisdom.

The Power of Hope

The first developmental crisis that confronts each infant between birth and one-and-a-half years old is trust versus mistrust of parents. If nurturing, warm, affectionate care is given, if the immediate environment and the parent figures are experienced as dependable, children learn to trust and consequently are optimistic. They become hopeful because their earliest significant parent figures are reliable and caring.

> "Life can only be understood backward, but it needs to be lived forward."
> —Soren Kierkegaard

Hope is the virtue or power that develops from the successful resolution of the internal conflict about whether it is safe to trust parents. Hope is the belief that certain wishes are attainable in spite of everything. Once established as part of the personality of the child, hope can later sustain a person even when trust seems unrealistic. The capacity to hope is at the center of being human. It is a feeling or belief that solutions to most problems are possible and that dreams for a better future have a chance of being realized.

When people are without hope, they lose interest in the future and often lose the energy to face even simple daily tasks. Of course, some things cannot be changed no matter how high the hope. At a time like that, trusting persons, in spite of unhappiness, still hope to make the best of the situation.

Some of these people may be overly trusting. They see the world through rose-colored glasses. Life may have been "ideal" when they were children, so they trust everyone and continue to trust them when clear evidence shows some people are not trustworthy. Gullible and naïve, unwilling to think critically about a person or situation, these people may collapse when they recognize the truth.

People who do not gain a basic sense of trust in infancy and thus develop the power of hope, may go through life feeling incomplete, empty, and distrustful of others. Those who do experience basic trust early in life may, in the process of growing up, lose it because of some tragedy or crisis. They may then live life feeling deeply lonely, wondering whether it is ever safe to trust again.

The inability to trust often leads to a pervading sense of depression that interferes with healthy development. Children who are abandoned, whether by death or desertion, also may lack the strength to trust and hope unless they have loyal substitute parents. Children who are consistently ignored, seldom touched, brutalized, or starved may not develop at a normal rate.

In later life, such people may expect others to ignore them or be untrustworthy in some other way. Because of this underlying fear, they may choose as spouse or friend someone who is actually trustworthy and then act in such negative ways that the other person leaves the relationship out of desperation. Or, without ample degrees of trust and hope, they may cling to someone from an overly dependent position that restricts their own freedom to develop autonomy.

The Power of Will

The necessary dependence during the first year and a half of life begins to moderate as children, moving toward age three, become aware of their emerging autonomy through the growing power to use their bodies. They discover they don't need to be carried; they can walk and do many other things on their own. They discover their will and the power of their will.

Children of this age are very ambivalent. They often do not want to let mother out of sight, yet they want to be independent when she is around. Along with this conflict between the urge for autonomy and the lingering inability to be autonomous comes self-doubt and shame for not being able to do things without help and for crying or "acting like a baby." In many families, boys are encouraged to be independent and girls are not. Both may be shamed by their parents if they act in a way deemed inappropriate by the parents.

Shame is experienced as a diffused sense of anxiety, self-doubt as not living up to a fantasized ideal. Both feelings are based on a decision that "I am weak or inadequate." This is toilet-training time, so it is not surprising that shame is often described as feeling exposed, "caught with my pants down." If the crisis of autonomy versus shame and self-doubt is not resolved, patterns of helplessness develop. Fear of trying new experiences may plague these people throughout life. This is not at all unusual for those who were hospitalized as young children. Their urges for physical independence and autonomy were severely restricted by hospital procedures, and their sense of safety was threatened when mother was not available.

If the crisis is successfully resolved, the strength to pursue happiness with less anxiety and more autonomy is developed. "I will do it," says the child. Developing a sense of will is crucial to breaking free and to achieving liberty. Will is determination to act in spite of self-doubt, in spite of shame that may be experienced if something is not done perfectly. The will acts as a self-organizing urge to set goals and motivate people to achieve them.

Children whose lives are overorganized by their parents may not learn how to recognize and use their wills. Later in life, their will is weak rather than strong. Either passively or anxiously, they may wait for destiny or fate or for some real or imagined authority to direct their lives. Even when their very existence is threatened, as in an earthquake or fire or when seriously ill or hurt, they may not know how to call on this inner power.

The power of the will is not the same as the will to power. The power of the will is based on using personal strength to take charge of one's own life. It is striving to do well and to actualize one's own potentials.

The will to power is based on efforts to take charge of someone else's life. It shows in one of two ways. A person may strive for power over others from a position of superiority (trying to be better than anyone else) in a class, on a job, in appearance, in social life. This person often shows high ambition or self-righteousness and uses power over others in the same way a controlling parent does.

The opposite type is the person who tries to control others through helplessness. This person may feel anxious and inadequate and thus act shy or weak, use poor judgment, or try to get others to make decisions. By acting helpless, this person also uses power—to manipulate others into caretaking roles.

The Power of Purpose

During ages three to seven, interest begins to shift from wanting autonomy to concern for "Who am I (as a boy or a girl)?" Awareness of one's sexual identity becomes important. Boys tend to seek their mother's attention; girls may act to get their fathers to notice them. Parents are often confused by a son's remark that "I'm going to marry Mama when I grow up" or a daughter's remark that "I wish Mama would go away so I could have Daddy to myself." Another difficult crisis exists for children who did not happen to be born the "right" sex to please their parents. They are in the constant process of deciding what kind of person to be and developing a sense of purpose for living.

When children's efforts at self-understanding and goal setting are misunderstood, punished, or ridiculed, they experience guilt. Guilt is not the same as shame. Shame is more likely to stem from a sense of inferiority at not being able to be autonomous. Guilt is experienced at not being able to please others. If a person often takes initiative and is disapproved, then the power to set goals that have purpose and meaning may be suppressed or seriously damaged.

When a child hears messages like "I'll decide what you should do and you better obey me," he or she may experience extreme feelings of guilt for breaking even minor rules. Children may stop thinking for themselves if they are criticized when they do so. They may develop a compulsive need to please others, and the "others" may not be willing to be pleased by anything less than perfection. Thus the purposeful goal-setting urges that develop in preschool years may be thwarted or distorted. For this person, goals that need to be self-determined may be difficult to decide upon in later life.

> *"Education is an ornament in prosperity and a refuge in adversity."*
> *—Aristotle*

If the crisis of initiative versus guilt is resolved, however, a person is able to take more initiative without feeling guilty, even if the initiated action is far from perfect. These people have a sense of *purpose* and know the power of it, and they have a conscience about using it. Life has meaning. Happiness is discovered through using the power of purpose to set and achieve realistic goals.

The Power of Competence

Between the ages of seven and twelve, the crisis of mastery versus inferiority emerges. The need for mastery arises in two areas. There is a need to master academic challenges and a corresponding need to master social challenges.

Mastery in academics is possible during these years because children are developmentally ready for active learning and are able to focus their attention. They are also more capable of social success at this age. All-boy groups and all-girl groups are typical. There is more freedom from home control and more chance to learn how to interact with others.

Children who are not successful in their efforts to master the academic and social challenges usually experience a painful sense of inferiority when they are out in the world. They feel very awkward instead of competent. If they feel awkward, they may withdraw from interaction with peers and become loners, using their time as bookworms or TV addicts. Later in life, such a person may have few (or no) friends, may work at something that calls for being alone, and may continue to feel inferior to others and not know what to do about it.

Some children who feel inferior begin to act in aggressive or delinquent ways, cutting school or failing academically. Later, they may continue delinquent behavior. Children who succeed socially and fail academically may continually seek out others. They may feel incompetent at making choices and may only do so with others who are willing to lead while they follow.

Building a sense of competence can be very difficult. For example, the person who feels inferior in academics may need to develop sports abilities or interests in various hobbies. The person who feels inferior in interpersonal relations may need to join some kind of program that provides opportunities for a gradual emerging of social skills. People with very high intelligence sometimes decide to focus their interests in areas in which they are most competent. They may recognize, painfully, that the number of people they can relate to at an intense intellectual level is not as high as they wish.

The Power of Fidelity

To affirm one's own identity and be loyal to it is the task for persons between the ages of twelve and eighteen. Unless this is done, a person may experience years of identity diffusion.

Adolescence is also a time when young people question traditional values and ask ideological questions about the meaning of life. The process of questioning values naturally includes questioning self-identity: "Am I a valuable person?" "Is it permissible to be who I am?" "Do I know who I am, or am I confused about my identity?"

One of the major reasons this period is so difficult, especially in some parts of the Western world, is that many adolescents are kept dependent—by law, society and parents—for an extended period of time. Their opportunities for growing up and taking their place in the adult world are restricted.

The sense of identity diffusion, "I don't know who I am," is a continuing problem if this crisis is not resolved. Drug abuse is only one sign that a healthy personal identity has not been achieved. Unwillingness to take responsibility for one's feelings and behavior is another. Blaming others is a third way. It implies that the blamer is outside the situation and not responsible for what goes wrong. Personal pleasure, regardless of its effect on others, may then become the major goal in life. A person's sexuality matures during these years, yet the capacity for authentic and caring love—for a partner or for children—may not develop because of identity diffusion and confusion.

Adolescence is a time in life when bodies and sexual urges are changing so rapidly that young people often feel confused about who they are and about the values and people that they want to remain faithful to. Rituals, such as a bar mitzvah, that recognize this stage in life are important. So, too, are parents who are affirming, not exploiting, and friends who are also affirming. Joining clubs, forming romantic relationships, and developing close friends are usually efforts in this direction.

When a firm sense of identity is established during these years, the power of fidelity is also established. This power is the ability to remain loyal to one's self and to others in spite of value contradictions that are sometimes confusing.

Fidelity is necessary for the next step, which is learning how to move into an authentic love relationship that is affirming. Without a strong sense of identity and the power of fidelity, feelings of loneliness and separation from the entire world may become overwhelming. Love may seem elusive, something at the end of a rainbow and always out of reach.

The Power of Love

Intimacy versus isolation is the next developmental crisis. It is related to unresolved issues around trust or nontrust which begin to surface again between ages eighteen and thirty. "Dare I trust someone enough to be truly intimate, or shall I withdraw and insulate myself instead?" "Am I important enough so that someone will come if I need them?" "Will they accept me as I am with all my unresolved needs?" "If I love other people, will they eventually leave me?"

One of the mistakes many people make when they form intimate relationships is to expect the other person to be trustworthy in every area of life, 100 percent of the time. That is seldom, if ever, the case. Everybody makes promises to themselves and others, and everybody breaks some of their promises. This happens by intent or by accident, and when it does, one person usually defends and justifies himself or herself by offering a "reason" for the broken promise. The other person defends and justifies his or her anger or despair. "I just couldn't help it" is a widely heard plea for forgiveness. "But you promised!" is the widely heard retort and plea for commitment.

The capacity to love, with a mutual devotion that can endure and reduce normal differences of opinions and antagonisms, grows more readily if the earlier trust issues arising from birth to one-and-a-half-years old have been resolved. Strongly based on awareness of personal identity and commitment to fidelity, love, as it develops between eighteen and thirty, is selective and is often experienced as a shared identity. Without love, life seems empty and hopeless, and loneliness seems inevitable.

People speak of love in many ways. They say they are "falling in love" or "falling out of love" or they speak of "making love" or "losing love." They speak of loving their cat or dog, their garden or car, their children, their spouse. However people may speak of it or define it, love is usually recognized as an intense emotion that gives pleasure and delight when it is reciprocal and leads to agony when it is not.

Love is often confused with romance, although they are not the same. Romantic love is usually short-term and an exaggeration of emotional highs and lows. It is somewhat manic-depressive. It's like being on a roller coaster going up to the peak of excitement then dropping suddenly. This kind of love can have a high cost.

Real love is more comprehensive. It may also have highs and lows, yet underneath both feelings is a steady current of trust and appreciation. Between some people, love involves sexual desire. Always it includes unconditional good will and the yearning for closeness that is part of intimacy. Love protects from the sadness of isolation and the terror of abandonment.

The freedom to be oneself and the happiness when sharing confidences and interests is lovingly experienced in the context of friendship. The happy person is one who counts both family and nonfamily members as friends and takes time and effort to cultivate and encourage the growth of friendships. Whereas idealism, romanticism, and adventure characterize friendships in youth, the reinforcing cement of love, without possessiveness, characterizes more mature relationships. In nonpossessive relationships, people keep their own identities and encourage others to do the same.

> *"It's a funny thing about life; if you refuse to accept anything but the best, you often get it."*
> —*Sommerset Maugham*

Because life without love reinforces negatives, it is important to assess one's friendships. Some people remain friends with others only if it is to their financial, social, or emotional advantage. Knowingly or unknowingly, they use others and, in the using, are often abusive of what the friend has to give. This is not friendship; it may give some mutual satisfaction, but the satisfaction is usually temporary. Eventually, the relationship begins to feel restrictive or boring to those involved, often because it has been based on use instead of on love.

The Power of Caring

Between the ages of thirty and sixty, the critical decision is whether to give parental care to others of a younger generation or whether to stagnate in self-indulgence. The successful resolution to this crisis is the development of the power of caring.

Generativity is the word for active concern for the next generation. This is not the same as having children. Some people who have children have little concern for them or for the world in which they live; they consider their children to be like attractive jewels for them to show off, or beasts of burden to be put to work doing chores.

Parents like this do not think about the human species as a whole. They do not accept the importance of children in the growth of a community, the importance of children playing, or the importance of children being with peers so that they can develop more social competence. They do not care about the next generation. Their primary concern is for themselves.

Sometimes when children grow up, move out of the home, and do not need their parents to the degree they did as children, the parents sink into depression. They suffer from identity confusion because their identity has been too closely associated with taking care of the family.

You don't have to give birth to children to offer the care

that is characteristic of generativity. Working with young people, being a good role model, or taking an active interest in the lives of young friends are all efforts at caring for the next generation. And, of course, those who care for the future of our planet—environmentalists, for example—are showing concern for the next generation.

Care is an ever-widening concern for others, not just family members. It may or may not involve physical caring out of a sense of duty. It does involve action. Truly concerned people who care are powerful people. They put their caring into action. They become involved in issues of social change and acknowledge people's rights to liberty and the pursuit of happiness. They have a healthy need to be needed, and a need to leave the world a better place for having been a part of its growing and healing.

When people are not willing to be involved in generativity by showing care for the next generation, they often find others are not concerned about them. Not caring, they become stagnant like marsh water without movement. They are progressively less interested in others, locked into self-absorption, self-pity, or self-adoration. Frequently, their only concern is for their own satisfaction, physical health, or financial wealth.

The Power of Wisdom

Ego integrity versus despair is the crisis that faces people after they reach their sixties. The person who has not solved this crisis is often preoccupied with self, fearful of death, and convinced that life has no meaning. Persons who have met this crisis recognize the value of their chosen lifestyles and take responsibility for what they have done, or not done, with their lives. They have ego integrity, which leads them to wisdom.

> *"Besides the noble art of getting things done, there is the noble art of leaving things undone. The wisdom of life consists in the elimination of nonessentials."*
> —Yin Yutang

Wisdom, the happy combination of knowledge and experience, includes the awareness that life is transitory and death a certainty. So the person of integrity continually searches for the meaning to be found in later years. Long-range achievement is no longer a high priority. Short-range achievable goals take precedence. Long vacations become less important than daily pleasures. With decline in bodily strength, the wise older person is able to utilize available psychological strengths to transcend some physical frailties. A sense of impermanence pervades life. Paradoxically, there is also a sense of permanence, with the awareness that the world will endure whether or not they are there to observe it.

In the process of developing ego integrity, wise elders still pursue liberty and happiness. They often discover a new spiritual dimension to life. They have accepted their parents and stopped blaming them. They've stopped blaming themselves for being who they are. With a sense of freedom, they may review developmental crises that were not resolved earlier and change what they can change while they have time. With new wisdom comes a more detached view of life. In the final years the challenge is to meet death with faith, dignity, and a new kind of freedom.

Positive Values with the Loss of Power

Powerlessness is generally thought to be a negative concept. But it is not always negative. Brief times of powerlessness may rejuvenate a person's body, mind, and spirit, much like a vacation does.

A period of hopelessness, about a job, a family member, or a living situation may lead to realistic appraisal and acceptance of a situation that cannot be changed. Mental and emotional energy can then be liberated for the development and pursuit of more satisfying and productive goals.

A time of self-doubt and overdependence can lead to analyzing one's knowledge and value systems. This may result in a new level of intellectual and physical autonomy (as, for example, when deciding to break out of a brutalizing situation). Self-doubt could lead a person to seek education or help from others.

When guilt is experienced, the positive value may be choosing to make amends. From another perspective, a person may discover that many guilt feelings are neurotic and inappropriate. This discovery can lead to taking more initiative in life, instead of waiting for others to set the goals.

Feeling incompetent occasionally can also be useful. If social skills were not mastered between the ages of seven and twelve or even later, a person is likely to feel inferior or shy with others. Observing how other people initiate or respond in social situations can help one develop new skills that increase chances for happiness. Feeling incompetent academically is so common and widely recognized that men and women increasingly return to schools and universities. Learning something new, or getting a longed-for degree, usually increases competence and decreases feelings of inferiority.

The discomfort of reexperiencing adolescent identity confusion often activates the desire for psychotherapy or, at least, introspection about what it means to be a woman instead of a girl, or a man instead of a boy.

Occasionally feeling distant from people, or feeling cold and hateful instead of warm and loving, leads to a crisis. The crisis is a symptom of the need to choose intimacy over isolation and to actively search for people with whom this might be possible.

A change from indiscriminately taking on responsibilities may allow a person to become more appropriately involved with self-interests. A new experience of self-care may lead to improved health and greater enjoyment, as well as a more accurate view of reality.

Despair, the opposite of hope, is counteracted by the ego integrity that leads to wisdom. Despair can lead to awareness that continuous integration is necessary, even in the later years of life. To integrate is to make whole. It is bringing the parts together, the parts of one's personality and the parts of one's total existence.

To be healthy is to recognize holiness as well as wholeness within oneself and the rest of the world. Recognizing holiness includes recognizing the rights all people have for life, liberty, and the pursuit of happiness with freedom, justice and peace.

Discovery Tools

Goal Setting in the Past

Consider the various times in your childhood, adolescence, and adulthood when you hoped for and actively pursued specific goals that you believed would make you happy. Perhaps you reached your goals, perhaps you didn't. Write about these times you recall, using the following prompts.

- Goals I have had:
- Methods I used to reach them:
- Degree to which I succeeded or did not succeed:
- Effect on my life at that time and now:

When you recall your goals and your pursuit of them, was it the achievements that were important, or was it the pursuit that you enjoyed?

- How long did your pleasure last?
- Are there implications for your life now?

Learning to Hope

Perhaps you can remember what your parents and parent figures and home and school environments were like when you were very young and whether you felt you could trust them or not, and what you hoped for or gave up hoping for.

- People who were trustworthy:
  Ways they showed it:

How this has affected me:
- People who were not trustworthy:
  Ways they showed it:
  How this has affected me:
- What I hoped for as a child:
  What happened to my hopes:
  How this has affected me:

Your Will and The Will for Power

As a young child, you were either encouraged or restricted from developing your will, which is the natural urge for independence and autonomy. How was this development encouraged or restricted?

- My attempts at autonomy:
- Encouraged or restricted:
- How I felt then:
- Effect on my life:

As a child, you also tried to exert your will to power over others by some form of manipulation, such as tears or temper tantrums. What was the result?

- How I tried to control others:
- How I succeeded or failed:
- How I felt then:
- The effect of my actions on self and others:

As you study your childhood patterns for using your will, are you satisfied? If not, what new-Parent messages do you need that could decrease your self-doubt and increase your independence?

From Guilt to Goal Setting

All children try to take initiative in various ways as they grow up. This is especially important between ages three and seven years. When not encouraged, children often feel guilty and begin to accept goals that please others instead of pleasing themselves.

- How I took initiative:
- Parent response:
- Effect on me:

In your current life, consider your goals, the purposes they serve in your life, and the initiative you take to achieve these goals.

- Goals I have established:
- Purpose of goals I have established:
- Initiatives I have taken to accomplish my goals:

In developing your new Parent, do you need increased encouragement to go for your goals? If so, what specific message do you need to give yourself?

From Inferiority to Competence

Between the ages of seven and twelve, you may have felt competent in some situations and incompetent or inferior in others. In this exercise, explore how you handled the basic academic and social challenges.

- Academic challenges in childhood:
- Achieved mastery or didn't:

- How I felt and acted:
- Effect on my life:
- Social challenges in childhood:
- Achieved mastery or didn't:
- How I felt and acted:
- Effect on my life:

Now consider your current intellectual and social challenges and note whether they are related to both your childhood urge for independence and your childhood attempts to master academic and social skills. How can a new Parent help you now?

- Current intellectual and social challenges:
- How they are or are not related to childhood:
- If I became a mentor, a coach or new Parent to myself, how might doing so help me in facing and dealing with intellectual and social challenges:

Identity and Self-Affirmation

In your teen years, you probably felt comfortable about yourself in some ways and not in others. Since then, you may have changed your mind, but how did you evaluate yourself at the time? Using the areas of concern below, list whether you were confused, somewhat uncomfortable, or accepting of yourself in your teen years.

- My appearance:
- My sexual identity:
- My capacity to think:

- My friendships:
- My home environment:
- My skills in sports:
- My skills in music:
- My skills in...:

If during your teenage years you were not comfortable with yourself, have you gained knowledge and appreciation of yourself since then?

If not, what do you need now from an internal and healthy new Parent, or a new coach or mentor figure?

From Loneliness to Intimacy

Loneliness is painful. It is first experienced in infancy. Usually, it is due to being isolated or ignored. When children's needs are not met and closeness to parents does not develop, a child does not learn how to trust. Mistrust and loneliness become unpleasant yet familiar feelings. In later life, loneliness is often expected. Intimacy may be avoided or restricted because of the early basic lack of trust.

- Specific people I wanted to be close to:
- What I did to encourage or avoid intimacy:
- The emotional effect of these relationships:

If you have a habit of developing relationships with others that do not last, is this related to some earlier issues around trust and mistrust?

- Do you select persons who are not trustworthy?
- Do you act in ways that alienate people?

If either of these are true, what could a new Parent tell you that could help you to could sustain love?

The Need for Balance

Whether to stay self-centered or reach out caringly to others is a question many people need to ask themselves. The opportunity comes especially in the middle years between ages 30 and 60.

Consider your current lifestyle and activities. Do you need to change your focus?

- My activities that are primarily self-centered:
- My activities that are primarily other-centered:
- Activities that involve both myself and others:

Is there a balance of some kind between what you do and how you act that is primarily for you and primarily for others?

If your activities and actions seem out of balance, what do you need from a new Parent to create balance?

To Be an Elder or to Be Elderly

The young find it almost impossible to comprehend what it is like to get old. Avoidance and denial are common barriers to thinking and planning for those years. When planning is done, it often is only in terms of having enough money and physical health to maintain life.

Historically, the title "elder" has been used for confidential advisors who are experienced and therefore valued for wise advice. Some cultures respect their elders and the wisdom they have accumulated; other cultures do not.

Some individuals or cultures seem to magnify the importance of money and productivity and deny the value of wisdom. However, as the so-called Baby Boomer generation gets older, that orientation may change.

Think of the various cultures (national, racial, family, etc.) you belong to. What views do they have about aging? Do you agree or disagree with these views? Why or why not?

If you want to be treated as an elder with wisdom, not just someone who is elderly, how can your new Parent assist you?

7

Self-Contracting for Happiness

Have you ever made a New Year's resolution, such as "I'll never do that again," and, within a week, done it again?

Or made a promise "I'm going to change myself beginning now" and then delayed and delayed for months on end?

Or made a contract that "I'm going to do it even if it's hard to do" and then completed the task ahead of schedule?

If so, you know whether or not you can trust yourself to keep the resolutions, promises, or contracts that you make. And, if you're like most people, sometimes you can and sometimes you can't.

A Look Ahead

This chapter deals with self-contracting—making a formal agreement with yourself to commit to some action, usually involving a change. Self-contracting means that you make a serious commitment with yourself, you build a contract, not just make a casual, halfhearted remark to yourself like, "Well, I'll give this or that change a stab" or "I'll send this change of actions in my life up and see if it flies." Reparenting involves serious, determined effort. In the ensuing sections, we will consider many aspects involved in self-contracting.

When people don't do what they agree to do, others begin to lose their trust in them. Perhaps you have lost your trust in someone else, or someone may have lost trust in you. You may also doubt the wisdom of trusting yourself. This uncomfortable feeling of being unable to trust may be momentary, it may exist only in some situations and not in others, or it may be pervasive. Whichever it is, this self-doubt can interfere with self-reparenting. To be effective, your new Parent needs to be consistently trustworthy and supportive of your growth. You have to keep your promises to yourself. You need to know you can trust yourself, whether those promises are little ones ("I won't cheat on my diet all day!") or big ones ("I'll stop being jealous!").

This chapter focuses on important issues: first, the nature of trust and how it develops and, second, how to trust yourself to make effective contracts with yourself that will put you on the road to happiness.

Thinking about the following three basic questions will accelerate your process.

- What do I want that would enhance my life?
- What do I need to do to get what I want?
- What would I be willing to do to achieve this?

Trusting Yourself

To trust people is to be able to depend on their integrity or ability. Learning to do this is the first crisis of early childhood, which, if resolved, leads to a sense of hope. Later in life, it becomes clear that some people are worthy of trust because they act with integrity and some are not. Knowing whom to trust and when to trust them is liberating and assists in the pursuit of happiness.

> "It is particularly incumbent on those who never change their opinion to be secure in judging properly first."
> —Jane Austin

Some people are basically trusting. They tend to trust everybody, including themselves. Others are suspicious or even despairing and trust nobody, including themselves. Others, usually with low self-esteem and a sense of inadequacy, do not trust themselves, although they may expect others to be trustworthy. People who only trust themselves believe other people are not dependable or capable enough.

These attitudes about trust may exist in varying degrees or at varying levels of intensity. For example, persons who are basically trusting may actually exaggerate their own and other people's commitments and capacities. They may see the entire world through rose-colored glasses and ignore problems that really exist. A different pattern is noticeable in persons who are always helping others. They may trust only themselves, refusing to believe that other people are competent and can usually direct their own lives.

People are fortunate if they have had other people in their lives whom they could depend upon and trust. Now, however, the focus is on being a trusting, responsible, motivating, and committed parent to yourself.

Contracting for success and knowing that success is possible requires an awareness of your own attitudes about trusting—an awareness of promises that have been kept and promises that have been broken—especially the promises made to yourself.

Problems of Inconsistency

Learning whether it is wise or not to trust parents is the first developmental crisis of childhood. If infants learn their parents can be trusted, they become able to hope. An attitude of hopefulness becomes part of their personalities and may last for a lifetime because of their early experiences.

Despair is the opposite of hope and inconsistency can lead to despair. A frequently heard lament is "I can't trust anybody; I can't even trust myself." Just how does this despair start?

If you had parent figures in childhood who were often inconsistent and did not do what they said they would do, you probably decided that you couldn't trust them. If that style of parenting became part of your Parent ego state, then you may be inconsistent in similar ways.

Another reason for lack of trust is if one of your parent figures was a promise breaker and another parent figure was just the opposite. In such cases, your commitment to yourself and others may fluctuate between indifference and perfection because of your role models.

Your new inner Parent needs to be consistently supportive of your potential for growth. It needs to encourage you as if you were part of a winning sports team. It needs to remind you that you are grown up and can keep promises or can stop making promises that you are uncertain about keeping.

Like lamps plugged into electrical outlets, old messages

can be unplugged. You don't need to listen to outdated messages. Your analytical, data-processing Adult part of your personality can help evaluate these messages. If you are functioning as a new Parent, or coach or mentor, to your inner Child, old messages do not need to direct your life unless you turn them on. The choice is yours.

If you choose to be more trustworthy and keep the healthy commitments you make to yourself, your inner Child will experience more peace. You will even sleep better at night and this can be a major step forward on the broad road to happiness.

Planning for Change

Becoming trustworthy requires admitting, at least to yourself, that something is wrong and that you have a part in it. That something wrong may be about your situation at home or work, about the way you think, feel, or act. It may be about a health problem or a career problem. The list of potential things wrong is endless.

After admitting to a problem, the question is whether or not the situation can be changed and if you can initiate the change. If both answers are affirmative, the planning period begins.

A plan usually involves specific decisions such as "I'm going to stay on my diet for one full week" or "I'll never again let myself explode in rage" or "From here on, I will keep my appointments instead of always making excuses for being late" or "I'm a fool to go to doctors if I don't follow through and take their advice, so I'm going to stop being a fool."

We often know what we want and know what we must do to get it. Yet, we avoid committing ourselves, especially if following through on a commitment means counting on others who may or may not be dependable.

It is uncomfortable to discover that we may be among those who cannot be counted on. For example, if we say we are going to clear off our desk and day after day make excuses for not doing so, we create our own discomfort with ourselves.

Contracting Theory

Being trustworthy to yourself so that you are able to give up habits that interfere with your happiness is a natural, healthy way to self-care. It will lead you to success in many areas of your life. Perhaps you want to be more successful in the financial part of your life, your sex life, your family life, your education, or some other area. If so, the area you are dissatisfied with may need a radical change or improvement. In addition, the positive changes you have already made may need to be reinforced so that they remain a strong, consistent part of you. Deliberate changes usually are based on self-contracts.

A contract is an agreement to do something about something, such as taking time out for a vacation or completing a project by a certain date or solving a problem that is creating too much physical or emotional stress.

Contracts are part of everyone's daily life. They can be legalized or not. Some contracts, such as marriage contracts or employment contracts, are legal contracts, and breaking them often requires the services of an attorney. Other contracts, such as completing a specific curriculum at school, making regular deposits to a savings account, or engaging in an exercise program are not regulated by law. Yet, the successful completion of these kinds of contracts usually increases a person's self-esteem. Completion also raises motivation and increases strength to make more contracts that will lead to further satisfaction.

> *"The secret of success is constancy to purpose."*
> —*Benjamin Disraeli*

Successful contracts made with yourself (self-contracting) need to be cooperative ventures. At least two parts of the personality need to agree that a change is desirable. The inner Child needs to be aware of wanting something that will lead to success and happiness. The logical Adult part of the personality needs to agree and (urged by the Child) to figure out if what is wanted is possible to obtain. Some things are impossible. The world won't fit on a silver platter regardless of how hard a person might want it that way.

Goal Setting for Success

Setting goals that will lead to more success is a major challenge in the pursuit of happiness. Many people set goals that cannot be met because they involve trying to get someone else to change. If the other person wants to change, well and good. If not, failure is inevitable.

The most successful goals are those which involve changing oneself. In self change, specific goals need to be established, then evaluated to see if they are practical and achievable. If not practical and achievable, the goals must be revised until they meet these criteria.

It is also important that progress moving toward a goal can be measured. If, for example, someone wants to cut down on smoking, it is necessary to state the goal in numbers: "I want to go from twenty cigarettes a day to five." If that person is courageous enough to cut back this much, he then will need to decide if he is willing to forfeit the five. It's not easy to break addictions. Sometimes a contract to improve one's life in some small way seems easier.

When goals are overly optimistic or impossible to reach or are not revised (the fate of many New Year's resolutions), they are not achieved. When resolutions are not kept, then previous beliefs about being inadequate or not being able to trust oneself are likely to be recycled. They get replayed like a badly scratched 78-rpm record that you listen to because it's familiar in spite of the poor sound quality.

Goals with the potential of success are those that are reasonable and practical and within a person's power to achieve. When the goals are achieved, the taste of success is sweet, the sound is grand, and the result is, at least, a moment of happiness.

Some people know their goals. They know exactly what they want. Others are not so sure. They just know they want to be happy. Pinpointing the area of life that is not satisfying often leads to the ability to focus on specific goals for improvement. So, the question is, "What do you want to enhance your life?"

Note, the question is not just "What do you want?" What we want may be bad for us or others. It may give us only momentary pleasure or be damaging to our lives instead of

enhancing them. Thus, we must be able to recognize wants that are positive, construc-
tive, and healthy. So, the question for goal setting re-ally is, "What do you want that will change your life for the better?"

> *"Courage is the capacity to move ahead in spite of despair."*
> —Rollo May

Designing Specific Goals

After determining the general area of life where change is wanted, the next step is to focus on specifics. For example, persons who are dissatisfied with their educational back-grounds may need to clarify and specify what they want instead. Do they wish they had studied in a different field or gone to a different school or applied themselves more seriously to the courses they took? They need to decide on specific goals that, if achieved, would make up for what they consider to be deficits in their education.

As another example, persons who are dissatisfied with their general physical health may need to be very clear and specific on what they want instead. Do they want to lose weight or gain weight? If so, how many pounds? They will also need to analyze themselves to determine whether they are motivated enough to keep their own commitments to some form of self-care such as dieting or exercising.

If you are dissatisfied with your family life or social life or sexual life, what exactly do you want instead? What goal and goal specifics would enhance your life and have the potential for success?

It is not enough to want to be happier. Happiness can be

in the planning, it can be in the pursuit, or it can come with achievement, but being happier takes goal specifics, commitment, and action.

If, time after time, people make promises to themselves and then break them, it means the promises have likely been built on grandiose expectations or insufficient commitment, not reality. Specific goals can only be reached if the expectations are reasonable and meet some of the needs and wants of the inner Child to be cared for and respected.

> *"Remember that not to be happy is not to be grateful."*
> —Elizabeth Carter

Time as a Basic Requirement

After deciding what would enhance your life and establishing a specific goal, a plan is needed. Before the plan is made, there are basic requirements to be met. These requirements include an awareness of the time available, the energy to be expended, and the level of motivation needed.

One of the most important requirements for reaching a goal is the capacity to use time effectively. People can use their time in the pursuit or enjoyment of success, or can misuse it so that most plans they make are doomed to fail.

Restructuring the use of time is sometimes hard because of the choices involved. Choice is often difficult. People who already fill their time in enjoyable and productive ways may not want to give up any current activities even for increased future enjoyment and productivity. Others who overplan and overschedule themselves fill their time in less enjoyable and less productive ways. Like jugglers who are able to keep many balls in the air at once until there are one too many balls, persons who overschedule usually feel driven or enslaved instead of liberated, happy, and successful.

Nonplanners of time represent a different type of person. Whether active or passive in behavior, these people prefer things to just happen. Some feel critical or resentful of people who plan how they are going to use their time. Others feel helpless when they compare themselves to those who use time productively. Unwilling to take charge of their own use of time, they passively resist changing themselves or responding to others who would encourage change.

Energy and Motivation

Successfully achieving your goals depends as much on generating sufficient energy and motivation to initiate and maintain action as much as it does on designing practical plans.

Change requires the expenditure of energy. Since everyone works with limited energy, the answer to the question "What must I do to reach my goal?" may seem overwhelming because of the energy needed simply to pursue your goal.

The use of personal energy can be blocked by law and tradition if personal goals are at cross purposes to those of society. So too, energy can be drained off by too much work or innumerable efforts to please others. Or, it can be interfered with by recurrent troubling thoughts.

When that seems to be the case, listening to the inner dialogue helps answer the questions: "How am I allowing my energy to be blocked?" "How am I allowing my energy to be drained off so I have little left to reach my goal?" "How am I allowing my anxiety or fear of success or failure to interfere with my planning for success?"

Another basic requirement before establishing a firm plan is generating the motivation to make the plan work or the motivation to revise it so that it will work. When people are motivated, they are stimulated to action. Self-motivation is based on the belief that the pursuit or achievement of a particular goal will give one's life more value. Motivation is related to values. If people value friendship, they find life to be meaningful when they are with friends. Thus, they structure their time and energy because of what they value. They know what they want, and they know what they need to do to get it.

The Need to Change Habits

Habits are learned patterns of behavior and involve consistent ways of thinking, feeling, and acting. Some habits, such as brushing your teeth, are positive and contribute to health; other habits are negative and can lead to poor health.

Many habits begin in childhood and, like addictions, are difficult to give up. Making effective contracts to change unwanted habits and trusting yourself to keep your contracts lead to success, even happiness.

Habits that do not lead to success can be changed for those that do. For example, some people escape from reality or from other people by watching too much television. It becomes a habit that may be given up by becoming more involved in study or sports or hobbies of some kind. Carelessness about exercise and eating or about personal hygiene and appearance, may be replaced by new habits that enhance health and good looks.

Habits can be changed in many ways. Sometimes, they are changed as a result of external pressure or encouragement from others. Sometimes, they change because of internal pressure or encouragement from oneself. When the external pressure "You should change, and you can do it" is congruent with the internal pressure "I want to change, and I am going to do it," people experience new energy and the capacity to trust themselves with a plan for action.

Negative habits are like chains. One link often leads to another. An alcoholic may be habit-bound to stop at the local bar on the way home. A TV addict may be habit-bound to collapse in front of the TV and emotionally withdraw from family or friends. A workaholic, after a long hard day, may be habit-bound to work even longer.

Overworking is often linked to self-pity or grandiose expectations. In such cases your new Parent may need to insist on your taking more time to relax or more vacations to break up the self-destructive habit.

By reprogramming yourself with a new inner Parent, you can change your old habits for new positive habits and become happier.

The Cost of Change

When a person establishes a particular goal and develops a workable plan to reach it, his or her next step is determining the cost during the pursuit and the cost when the goal is reached. There is always a cost.

Sometimes the cost is financial, for example, when you pay a tuition fee for further study. Sometimes the cost is physical, as when you get less sleep while working and going to school. Sometimes the cost is emotional, such as feeling conflict because a spouse is critical of the time, energy, and money spent by the one who wishes to study. In any case, when a goal is chosen and the requirements for reaching the goal are clear, the cost often becomes apparent and it must be reckoned with. In most instances, at least part of the cost is experienced as stress.

Many people are unable or unwilling to pay the cost to strive for a goal. They are not willing to do what they need to do for whatever reason. When they discover this, they need to revise their goal or choose a different goal for which they have a higher level of motivation. They need to decide whether they want to use their will power, whether they will continue to procrastinate, or whether they will let anxiety and self-doubt rule their lives. They need to know the potential cost and, if tolerable, set out courageously with a sense of self-trust.

The Possibility of Sabotage

We may deliberately or without awareness, sabotage ourselves. People often choose unique ways for undermining their goals. A person on a special diet who is planning to go to a six-course dinner party might go to lunch that same day at a restaurant where the food is served in large proportions. Another, with plans to go to a big football game to relieve stress, may wait until the last minute before leaving work, and, in his rush, forget to take the tickets. In both examples, they sabotaged their own goals.

During the self-reparenting process, one way to sabotage oneself is to replay, time and again, old negative parental messages from childhood. These replays delay success and sometimes lead to failure.

Some people worry about being successful because they believe that others will be jealous of their success. That may be true. Others may in fact become jealous or resentful or angry.

> *"LOST, yesterday somewhere between sunrise and sunset—two golden hours, each set with golden minutes—no reward is offered for they are gone forever."*
> —Horace Mann

Accepting that as a possibility, or even a probability, can be liberating. Dwelling on this can be enslaving and can interfere with the successful pursuit of happiness. This can easily be a form of subconscious sabotage.

Another example of sabotage is the gradual undermining of a goal that occurs when one continually entertains internal arguments about why the goal is not worth the cost. Like the foundation of a building that slowly weakens because of underground water, unwillingness to remain consistently firm with yourself erodes both your progress and your ability to observe and process information. Freedom of action and purpose may collapse and worse situations arise that are even costlier to overcome.

Refusing to be a consistent, trustworthy new Parent to yourself is the easiest way to undermine potential success.

Therefore, it is necessary to know in what areas of life you can trust yourself and in what areas you are not trustworthy. Do you keep your promises to yourself or sabotage your goals as you work to achieve them?

Knowing your potential for sabotaging your own goals will help you fight against these tendencies.

Success Shows

Success is not something that is easily hidden. It shows in many ways. Sometimes it can be seen in someone's improved health—in the new sparkle in the eyes or the bounce in the walk. Sometimes it shows in a changed lifestyle, in the better use of time and the enjoyment of both work and play. Sometimes it shows in the use of money, finally spending it wisely instead of with credit-card impulsiveness or miser-like hoarding. Sometimes success shows in changed relationships with others. Destructive relationships may be discarded and life-enhancing relationships may be developed and cherished. Success shows in any area of life when goals to improve that part of life are established and achieved.

It is important to be clear on how you will know when you reach your goal. The achievement of some goals is obvious. For example, if you are going for a university degree, your goal will obviously be reached when you get your diploma. If you are applying for a new job, your success will show when you get it. If your goal is to lose weight, you will know you have been successful when you buy clothing that is a smaller size. However, the achievement of other goals may be far more difficult to determine. For example, if you have self-contracted with yourself to show less anger over small annoyances in life or if you are attempting to change your relationship with your children to create more positive communication, these goals will often be matters of subjective interpretation. Create signposts—such as a full week without falling back into negative patterns—on your route to success so that you will recognize progress toward your goals.

> *"The toughest thing about being a success is that you have to keep on being a success."*
> —*Irving Berlin*

Reward yourself with a smile when you manage to keep one of your contracts. In fact, why not tell someone else about it who will join you in a smile, give you a pat on the back, and offer praise?

When Others Judge

Knowing what your strong and weak points are in relationship to how you respond to people, especially when they judge you critically, is important knowledge to have when establishing contracts for success.

Some people set goals and make contracts that are much lower than necessary because they are afraid that others will be jealous or will avoid them if they succeed. They may think it is disloyal to be more successful than others in their family.

Many people are deeply afraid of being criticized, usually because of experiences in childhood. Even when they become competent adults, some still imagine criticism will turn into brutality, as it once did, or they imagine criticism implies that another will withdraw his or her love.

In any case, they see others as both judge and jury. They tend to see themselves as misunderstood victims. Solving this problem requires analyzing potential prejudices of others to decide who it is safe to tell about your goals and when it is wiser to be silent.

Let your new caring Parent use some of its mentoring and teaching skills to help you reaffirm your efforts and to allow you to understand that the successful accomplishment of your goals for change should not be stalled by your concerns about the attitudes of others or by their efforts to discourage you. Talk to your new inner Parent and listen to the new possibilities you now possess.

A First-Aid Kit for Emergencies

It is not unusual for people to suddenly feel angry or confused or depressed while making changes and paying the costs of changing. When this occurs, it is useful to have the fantasy equivalent of a first-aid kit.

Perhaps this first-aid kit would include permission to go to a movie or have a leisurely dinner or long bubble bath or listen to favorite music or read a favorite book or visit an art gallery or phone a friend. Some people put objects they enjoy, such as candy or music CDs, into a box labeled "First-Aid for the Blues." Others put in pictures of people they love or an extra $20 to spend on a special treat. We all have developed ways of surviving and getting ourselves through the storms of life. What might help you in an emergency?

One of the most effective tools you could put into your emergency kit is the phrase "At least…" These words would then be followed by something positive, such as, "At least the weather is good today" or "At least I passed the examination with flying colors even if the preparation for it was exhausting" or "At least I have a decent job even if I don't get the one I want" or "At least I have friends to call when I am lonely." And, don't forget to include this one: "More than 'at least,' I actually am alive. I have life. I have the liberty to contract with myself to continue to pursue happiness." It's never too late.

Discovery Tools

Promises, Promises

During your life, you have probably made many promises to yourself that you may or may not have kept. The ways you kept or did not keep your promises reflect some of your strengths or weaknesses. In your notebook or journal, list the following.

- Promises I made to myself*:*
- How I managed to keep them*:*
- Excuses I used for breaking them*:*
- My excuses were valid or not valid because:

The excuses you used for breaking your promises may have been valid if the promises were unrealistic because the goals were not achievable.

The excuses you used that were invalid reflect the need

for a firmer new Parent, perhaps a tough Parent instead of a permissive one.

Write how you feel about the possibility of needing a firm new Parent who will insist on your keeping your promises to yourself.

Awareness of Requirements

Think of a project you would like to undertake, then assess it in terms of the time, energy, and motivation you will need to complete it.

- What are the approximate number of hours (per day, week, or month) that would be needed?
- I have that time available, or I could make that time by restructuring my current use of time (yes or no). (If you don't have enough time, then select a different project.)
- The energy that would be required is (possible or impossible) for me. (If impossible, select a different project.)
- My level of motivation to start and complete the project is (low or high). (If low, then select another project.)

With each goal you establish, continue to ask yourself about the requirements of time, energy, and motivation.

A Tentative Plan

The successful achievement of a goal usually requires a plan of action and a decision to start. Before that time, a tentative plan is often useful. Jot down answers to the following.

- What I want is:
- The resources I already have are:

- My first step would be:
- I could take that step on:
- Then I would:
- I would evaluate the plan in process by:
- My new-Parent response to this tentative plan might be:

Realistic and Measurable Contracts

To be successful, contracts must be clear, precise, and direct. They also need to be based on realistic and practical goals.

List a number of things you would like to have or places you would like to go or ways in which you would like to change. Then evaluate the following.

- Is each of these a realistic goal to pursue?
- How could I measure my progress toward each of these goals?

Be aware that what you want may not be what your parents of the past wanted you to have. If that is the case, your new Parent should help you to deliberately increase your motivation.

Habits to Keep or Change

You already know many of your habits, such as the processes you go through when you wake up in the morning or before you go to bed at night.

This particular exercise is to increase your awareness of how these contribute to or interfere with your happiness.

Make a list of habitual ways you act, think, or feel when

at home, at work, and in social situations. For each habit you list, note what you like about this habit and, if you need to change it, why.

- Habitual pattern:
    I like this about me because:
    I need to change this because:

What Do I Want That Will Enhance My Life?

Review the exercises in chapter 5 (pages 123–124) on the needs and wants of your inner Child. Start with some small goals that you could achieve if you decided to exert the time and energy. Be specific.

- Things I want or need that would enhance my life:
- What an encouraging new Parent would say about these wants and needs:

What Do I Need to Do?

Consider the areas in your life that you would like to change. Then focus your attention on a specific change and determine whether you would be really committed to that goal.

Write down a specific goal you want to achieve, then list below it the answers to the following.

- What I need to do to reach this goal:
- What unanticipated conflicts might arise which could prevent me from reaching this goal:
    - I would restructure my time by:
    - I would focus my energy by:

- My motivation to reach this goal is:
- Therefore, I conclude:

Reducing Anxiety

Becoming less sensitive about the insignificant matters or perceived slights in life can occur relatively quickly due to a new decision, or it may be a gradual process. Either way, becoming less sensitive to these things can liberate you to live more fully.

- List those things you are overly sensitive about (such as being evaluated or criticized) or objects or situations you unreasonably fear (such as being alone in your home on a dark night or being physically ill).
- How my life would be different if I weren't so anxious or afraid:

Now select one of the things you are overly sensitive about or one of the things you fear and design a plan for desensitization. Let the encouraging, loving new Parent you have developed help you plan, so that putting the plan into action will not be too threatening or too hard for you.

- One of my anxieties is:
- What I need to do about it is:
- The time and place to begin is:
- Helpful messages I need from my new inner Parent are:

What Am I Willing to Do?

You know what you want to enhance your life and what you need to do to get it. Now the question is, Are you willing to pay the cost?

- One goal I want to reach is:
- Briefly, what I need to do to reach the goal is:
- What I am willing to do is:
- The costs of pursuing this goal are likely to be:
- The costs of not pursuing this goal are likely to be:
- Therefore, I am (willing or not willing) to pursue this goal. (If you are not willing, choose another goal, or revise this one and repeat this drill until you define a life-enhancing goal that you have the motivation to pursue.)

How Will Others Respond?

Most people need some form of encouragement from other people when they are in the process of changing. However, be careful of talking about a potential change to someone who will offer inappropriate advice or who will criticize your goals.

- Name three people you might tell:
- Anticipate their probable responses:
- Would their responses help or hinder you:
- Therefore, I will or won't tell:

When self-contracting, it is often effective to tell others, whose opinions you respect, about your new commitment. So, ask your emerging new Parent to advise you on whom to tell.

ℬ

Celebrating Your Success

Did you ever want to give a celebration party or want to go to one, but felt too socially awkward to do so?

Did you ever want to celebrate with all your family and friends, but the timing wasn't right?

Do you ever fantasize a celebration you might give that couldn't be any fun so nobody would want to come to it?

When you think of the future, do you look forward to celebrating your successes and your new opportunities for happiness or not? If not, why not?

These questions are all concerned with time—past and future. But *now* is the time you are living. Now is influenced by past positive and negative experiences and, in turn, can influence what happens in your future.

A Look Ahead

Celebrating is one way to reinforce a decision to live now and to live with courage and zest. It is more than just expressing energy. In expressing energy, you can hang on to and reinforce negative experiences and feelings of the past. Or, you can use some of your energy positively, for instance, to forgive your parents who were not perfect and also to forgive yourself for being human and not perfect.

You can plan happiness now. You can celebrate who you are, what you have done with your life so far, and what you intend to do in the future. The right to pursue happiness and celebrate success is yours.

Life as a Movable Feast

Children don't like to be mistreated by their parents. Parents, being people, don't like being mistreated, either. Your new Parent is still very new. Treat it with courtesy and respect and with acceptance and love, and you will be treated the same. Your life will be richer, your liberty more extensive, your success and happiness greater.

As you continue to become more integrated and whole, each part of you will need positive reinforcement. You will need opportunities for joy and laughter as well as intellectual challenges that will stretch your mind. You will need friends who are fun and thoughtful and nourishing and sometimes you will need to celebrate with them.

Although life contains inevitable suffering, it can also be like a movable feast where each day you discover something large or small that calls for celebration. The causes are innumerable: sunrises and sunsets, moonlight and stars, the first spring flowers or first fall of snow, the call of the wild geese, the sound of the surf, the smell of the prairie, the crackle of a fire on the hearth, the touch of soft wind on the skin, the sweet taste of melon in your mouth. These sensory delights cost little—only awareness and the decision to enjoy them.

There are other causes for celebration that are interpersonal and include a more complex and satisfying response than the mere celebration of the senses: the snap of a fish on the line, the welcoming bark of a dog, the loving smile from a child, the unexpected letter from a friend.

There are moments when you may spontaneously celebrate alone. Finding your glasses or date book that had been lost for a week is something to cheer about. So is finding yourself and your uniqueness.

Celebrating may be a simple, brief moment and cost nothing, like hugging yourself or phoning a friend. It may be experienced as a high moment of delight or as a short prayer of relief and thanksgiving. You may choose to celebrate with a party or a vacation.

Whatever the cause of your happiness, time and space will be irrelevant when the moments occur. The past and future will be felt in the present. So, if you consider your life as a whole, and the liberty you have to enjoy it as being like a movable feast, your moments of happiness will increase and so will your reasons to celebrate.

Celebration Takes Many Forms

Birthdays, anniversaries, graduations, job advancement, or the birth of a child are only a few of the causes for celebration. They are celebrated in many ways—with cake and candles, presents and games, cocktail parties, special music, gifts, or favorite foods.

Celebrations may be highly organized, like a parade with bands playing, groups marching, and flags waving to honor a national holiday. Or, more spontaneously, they may take the form of a beer party for a few people after a sports event. They may involve thousands of people, as when peace is declared after a long war, or two people, celebrating a promotion. In every case, the merrymaking proclaims something important has happened and that people have the right to be happy.

People design celebrations according to cultural norms. One person's retirement party may include the traditional presentation of a gold watch and a dinner party. Another's may involve a picnic with balloons, music, and lighthearted dancing on the beach.

In order to celebrate, it is sometimes necessary to change habitual ways of responding to friends, colleagues, and family members. Occasionally, it may seem best to break off relationships or, at least, spend less time with critical or depressing people who stand in the way of your celebrating your change and growth. Spending less time with these people may allow you to develop new relationships that are friendly, growth-enhancing, responsible, and conducive to happiness.

Losing the Energy to Celebrate

Instead of celebrating, many successful people hide their successes. They refuse to celebrate and to feel happy, frequently using one of the following excuses: Their success is not really important and they may be ridiculed or ignored; their success will make someone jealous, and a friendship or work relationship may be harmed; they will be expected to perform still another task, and to perform it even more successfully; they are angry at someone or at a situation or even angry at the world; they fear it might take too much time away from their pursuit of other goals; they feel they do not deserve recognition and joy, either because they have failed in some other way or because "anything good that happens is just luck."

> "Small cheer and great welcome makes a merry feast."
> —Shakespeare

Regardless of what excuse a person may use, avoiding celebration is a denial of the potential excitement of living. Feelings of happiness that well up from a person's inner core deserve recognition.

Unfortunately, people often avoid celebrations because they have experienced a loss of energy. They feel so debilitated that they do not expect to enjoy celebrating. It is important to recognize that whether or not you will enjoy a celebration is often not a matter of energy, but a matter of choice.

Sometimes not enjoying a celebration is normal. When people are shocked by bad news or are seriously ill, celebrations become low priority. People often need and want to conserve energy to cope with the stress they are experiencing.

In some cases celebrations need to be postponed. Yet, at other times, just looking around to see how much there is in life to feel good about will provide the energy needed to celebrate.

Energy for celebrating may be especially low when traditions are too restrictive and act like a dam holding back energy. In many families and cultures there are laws or customs that spell out the details of celebrations. Like dams, customs may restrict the free flow of energy until pressure builds up and a break occurs. People can choose not to allow this to happen. They can choose to change some of the restrictive customs. Or, if the customs can't be changed, people can change their responses to them. Instead of feeling bound, their energy can flow freely. A good new Parent would encourage this.

> *"We must learn to be still in the midst of activity and to be vibrantly alive in repose."*
> —Indira Gandhi

In today's world of increasing cross-cultural families and multicultural workplaces, if people from one culture hold on vociferously to the beliefs and lifestyles with which they grew up, they are likely to miss opportunities to discover other forms of happiness.

People experience a loss of energy when they are continually drained by the demands they put upon themselves or accept from others. They won't say "no." They habitually put others first, try to please everyone, and do more than their share of work. These people are likely to prepare too hard for a celebration and become so stressed out that they don't enjoy it, or they don't get enough rest before a celebration. Afterward, having met too many obligations, they feel drained.

They could choose to say "no" to some demands made upon them. They could work easy instead of hard. They could take more time to enjoy life and to avoid feeling drained. They could be assertive on behalf of themselves. A good new Parent would encourage this.

Anxiety lowers energy levels. Many events cause anxiety and doubt. Parties, in particular, seem to bring out high levels of stress and anxiety in some people. They may worry about their appearance, the refreshments, what the neighbors might think, or who to invite. Worrying unnecessarily depletes energy and often doesn't leave us capable of enjoying ourselves.

The desire to be perfect is also energy depleting. People can choose. They can remind themselves that nothing has to be perfect. Joy is not based on perfection. It is based on being open to the wonders of the universe and to the wonders of relationships. A good new Parent will encourage this openness.

Deciding to Forgive

Forgiveness is the granting of pardon without holding resentment. It is not just saying "I forgive you." It is more than that. It is giving up resentment, anger, hate, and even self-righteousness. It is forgiving the humanness of others as well as your own humanness. Forgiving your parents is recognizing that they were influenced by their parents and culture, even as you were. Forgiveness, however, does not preclude regretting that life was not different for you and for them.

The ability to think clearly and act rationally and lovingly is immediately increased when people decide to forgive their parents and others. The energy to celebrate life is also increased when people let go of resentment and anger and forgive themselves for what they have done in the past.

Give yourself the present of forgiving yourself and others and watch your happiness grow.

All young people make decisions about themselves, about other people, and about how the world is or should be. Many people, however, do not alter their original decisions. They cling to them in spite of evidence that shows the decisions to be faulty or circumstances to have changed. If they become aware of having made faulty decisions, they can change them—sometimes by desensitization techniques, sometimes by re-education, sometimes by redecisions.

> "Children begin by loving their parents. Later they judge them. Sometimes they forgive them."
> —Oscar Wilde

Redeciding something is often needed to solve problems related to parents. This is a common issue brought to counselors and psychotherapists. One of the most effective ways to increase energy and to continue developing is to decide to forgive your parents and parent figures who were less than perfect. It is most effective when forgiveness is both intellectual and emotional. The resulting release of tension frees energy. It is as if the slate is wiped clean, and the day is new and fresh without the pollution of the past.

There are many ways to go about the process of forgiving one's parents. Some people use meditation to quiet themselves and let go of resentment. Some pray for the strength to forgive and often experience a change in attitude, with more acceptance of their parents.

Another common way is using role-playing techniques and replaying with emotion early childhood scenes, then replaying them again with a different sequence or ending. Other people use a cognitive thinking, intellectual approach. In doing so, they begin to recognize that the early lives of their parents could have been very troublesome. The parents of their parents could have had severe problems and have also felt enslaved. With this, they begin to recognize that finding fault is sometimes an excuse to avoid personal responsibility.

Dialogic self-talk, between the inner new Parent and inner Child, is an effective way to remind oneself that a lifetime of resentment has no positive value. Letting go of resentments is a sign of wisdom.

Laughter: The Medicine That Heals

Just as forgiving oneself and others is curative medicine and cause for celebration, healthy laughter activates the chemistry for the will to live. It often reflects joy and insight, attracts friends and lovers, breaks tension in uncomfortable social situations and seemingly increases the capacity to fight against disease. By expanding the chest and increasing respiration, laughter relaxes the body and helps stimulate good health. Laughter also releases the capacity to enjoy other people, because the universal ability to play, to create, and to have fun is liberating.

One of the signs of good mental health is the capacity to laugh at yourself. A healthy laugh is not a laugh of ridicule. It can be a laugh of insight when the cause or the solution to a problem is suddenly clear. It can be like the laugh of pleased parents who are enjoying the first steps of a child. It can be a laugh of delight between friends or an invitation between lovers.

What people laugh at differs from century to century, from culture to culture, and even from one stage of life to another. And, part of being human is accepting the fact that what is funny to one person is often not funny to another. Yet healthy, open-minded laughter is contagious, and healthy laughter celebrates the right to happiness.

Do you remember a time when you watched a funny movie or read a funny story? Do you remember how good your body felt after a deep laugh? Do you remember how clearly you experienced yourself and the rest of the world at that time?

These experiences are easy to reproduce. You can choose to laugh. Even if nothing is funny, you can laugh and your body will feel more relaxed. When you laugh, you will feel less emotional tension. You can laugh at all the absurdities of life—even at yourself. A good new Parent will encourage you in healthy laughter.

Messages From Your New Parent, Coach, or Mentor

Along with laughing and celebrating, please love yourself and take care of yourself. You will probably outlive your parents and other parent figures. The boldness of your youth may mellow like fine wine, your values may change, your lifestyle alter. Loss, loneliness, and sorrow are possible at any time, and that's the bad news. The good news is that joy and laughter and experiencing the wholeness of life while feeling part of all creation is also possible. You can choose. It's not too late.

As you choose, please choose happiness on an hour-to-hour, day-by-day basis, along with your plans for future happiness. Happiness is a peak experience, a high point. It's worth the struggle. Even though you are sometimes unhappy, remember you have been able to survive, so it's never too late to be happy.

Discovery Tools

Energy and the Zest for Life

The zest for life is a positive energy that enhances our days and leads us to enjoy life as it is or to strive for something more.

For this exercise, relax for a moment, take a few slow breaths, and let yourself reexperience times when you felt high positive energy and the zest for life. Then consider what was involved and why you think you felt that way.

- Situations when I felt high positive energy:
- Why I felt that way:
- What I did with my energy:

Now consider the times when your energy was low or negative and life did not seem worth living.

- Situations when I felt low energy or very negative:
- Why I felt that way:
- What I did with my energy:

How Can I Celebrate? Let Me Count the Ways

One way to evaluate yourself and your opportunities for enjoyment is to think in terms of your own "life, liberty and pursuit of happiness."

In this exercise, become aware of what you do celebrate

and what you don't: Your life (your good health)? Your liberty (an unexpected day off from work)? Your pursuit of happiness (enjoying new friends)? Jot responses to the following in your notebook or journal.

- Some of the ways I currently celebrate my life are:
- Some of the ways I currently celebrate my liberty are:
- Some of the ways I currently celebrate my pursuit of happiness are:

Consider your responses. What are you celebrating? Are you missing out on some chances for joyful celebration?

If so, what specific advice would an ideal new Parent give you?

Energizing Yourself

In this exercise, think about your river of energy and its flow. Be aware of how you can release your energy so it isn't blocked or drained off or restricted.

- Customs or traditions that block my energy:
     What I could do about them:
      What I'm willing to do about each one:
- People, tasks, or situations that take too much energy:
     What I could do about each one:
     What I am willing to do about each one:
- Anxieties that interfere with my free-flowing energy:
     What I need to do about each one:
     What I'm willing to do about each one:

As you reflect on the above, how about planning a little

celebration for yourself just because you are releasing your energy to pursue happiness and to celebrate it.

Forgiving Your Parents

This exercise is not for everyone. Forgiving parents who were less than ideal isn't absolutely necessary, but people who do so are likely to feel happier than those who carry around a grudge. Some readers may not need to forgive their parents for not being perfect because they have already done so. Yet, if any resentment remains, this exercise will help.

Pick a quiet time when other people are not around. Place two chairs facing each other and sit in one.

Relax, take a few deep breaths, close your eyes, and visualize one or both of your parents sitting opposite you.

Start a conversation with one or both by explaining how you have stayed resentful for so long. Then listen to what they say. If you feel comfortable doing so, move to the other chair and role-play your parents speaking to you.

Continue the dialogue and let your feelings emerge (perhaps grief or anger). Don't be afraid of your feelings; they belong to you and are under your control.

As you continue the dialogue, you may experience the pain in your parents' lives that influenced them to be the way they were. If so, try to understand and perhaps let yourself feel compassion. Compassion may lead to forgiveness.

Now write a short note of forgiveness to them, whether they are alive or dead. In the note explain the value of forgiveness and how it releases you to find serenity, new energy, and happiness.

Forgiving Yourself

Any celebration you have may turn out superficial or even dismal if you have not forgiven yourself. Many people find it all too easy to remember their own errors of judgment and their own improprieties.

If you have some of this unfinished business, think of something you are ashamed of. Then ask yourself the following questions. Jot your answers in your notebook or journal if you like.

- Have I made amends as best I could? If not, why not?
- If so, why am I unwilling to forgive myself?
- How would my life be different if I did?

Now start an inner dialogue with your encouraging new Parent and listen to the advice. Stop hanging onto the misery of the past.

Hold out your hands in front of you and shake them hard. Experience the process of letting go.

Write yourself a letter telling yourself it is finished, that you forgive yourself and that you are going to stop being so critical of yourself. Make a new self-contract, keep it, and get on with life and happiness.

Celebrating With Joy

Joy is usually accompanied by smiles and laughter. In this final exercise, experiment with ways to get people to laugh with you—just for fun.

Get a humorous book, go see a friend, and share something you find funny in it. Read it aloud to your friend and let yourself laugh. Try a chuckle, a guffaw, or a giggle. See what happens.

Phone another friend and talk about something funny that's happened to you. Maybe your friend will have a humorous incident for you.

Get a small group together and do a chuck-a-belly exercise for fun. In this, people lie down in a line and put their heads on the stomachs of the next person. Laughter starts at one end of the line and builds up. Tension is reduced and a sense of community is experienced.

Have a party and dress up in funny clothes, like a come-as-you-aren't party; get a funny game going or sing some funny songs or tell some limericks. Play charades. Laugh, enjoy, and celebrate. Your new Parent-Coach-Mentor is on your side and is in favor of the pursuit of happiness.

Last But Not Least

Use your new Parent and consider the three roles that can be played. In the role of the ideal parent, your new Parent can set limits and be gentle, loving, potent yet sympathetic. In the teacher-mentor role your new Parent can tell you to continue with your education, formal or otherwise. And, in the coaching role, your new Parent can encourage your physical health and your determination to succeed in the game of life, whether alone or on a team.

Reprogram yourself. Remind yourself that it's never too late to be happy. Even if things sometimes go wrong, say to yourself "You can do it. You've done it before, so pick yourself up and get going!"

Selected Bibliography

Beck, M.D. Aaron T. *Cognitive Therapy and Emotional Disorders.* New York: New American Library, 1976.

Benson, M.D. Herbert, and Marg Stark. *Timeless Healing: The Power and Biology of Belief.* New york, Simon and Schuster, 1997.

Bowlby, John. *Attachment and Loss, VOL. I.* New York: Basic Books, 1969.

Bowlby, John. *Attachment and Loss, VOL. II. Separation Anxiety and Anger.* New York: Basic Books, 1973.

Brown, Barbara B. *Supermind: The Ultimate Energy.* New York: Harper & Row, 1980.

Burns, M.D. David D. *Feeling Good.* New York: New American Library, 1980.

Cousins, Norman. *Anatomy of an Illness as Perceived by the Patient.* New York: W. W. Norton, 1979.

Cousins, Norman. *The Pathology of Power.* New York, WW. Norton, 1987.

Elias, Norbert. *The Civilization Process: The Development of Manners.* Translated by Jephcott Edmund. New York: Urizen Books, 1978.

Ellenberger, Henri. *The Discovery of the Unconscious: The History and Evolution of Dynamic Psychiatry.* New York: Basic Books, 1970.

Erikson, Erik. *Childhood and Society.* 2d ed. New York: W.W. Norton, 1963.

Fielding, Elizabeth. *The Memory Manual.* Clovis, California: Quill Driver Books, 1999.

Fiore, Neil A. *The Road Back to Health.* New York: Bantam Books, 1984.

Fraiberg, Selma. *The Magic Years.* New York: Scribner, 1959.

Freedman, Daniel. "Ethnic Differences in Babies." *Human Nature,* January, 1979.

Freud, Anna. *Infants Without Families.* New York: International Universities Press, 1944.

Gardner, Howard. *Frames of Mind: The Theory of Multiple Intelligences.* New York: Basic Books, 1983.

Gaylin, M.D. Willard. *Feelings.* New York: Ballantine Books, 1979.

Gilligan, Carol. *In a Different Voice.* Cambridge: Harvard University Press, 1982.

Harlow, H.F. *Learning to Love.* New York: Ballantine Books, 1971.

Herron, R.E., and B. Sutton-Smith. *Child's Play.* New York: Wiley, 1971.

His Holiness the Dalai Lama and Howard Cutler, M.D. *The Art of Happiness.* New York, Penquin Putnam, 1998.

Horney, Karen. *Neurosis and Human Growth.* New York: Norton, 1950.

Horney, Karen. *The Neurotic Personality of Our Time.* New York: Norton, 1937.

James, John, and Muriel James. *Passion for Life: Psychology and the Human Spirit.* New York: Penguin Books, 1991.

James, Muriel. *Marriage is for Loving.* Reading, Mass.: Addison-Wesley, 1979.

James, Muriel. *What Do You Do with Them Now that You've Got Them.* Reading, Mass.: Addison Wesley, 1974.

James, Muriel, and Dorothy Jongeward. *Born to Win: Transactional Analysis and Gestalt Experiments.* Reading, Mass.: Addison-Wesley, 1971.

James, Muriel. "Therapy Doesn't Always Hurt" *Perspective in Transactional Analysis.* Oakland, CA.: ITAA Press, 1998.

Kagan, J. *Developmental Studies of Reflection and Analysis.*

Cambridge, Mass.: Harvard University Press, 1964.

Kohlberg, L., and E. Turiel, eds. *Recent Research in Moral Development.* New York: Holt, Rinehart & Winston, 1972.

Lazarus, Arnold, and Joseph Wolpe. *Behavior Therapy Techniques.* Oxford: Pergamon Press, 1966.

Leboyer, Frederick. *Birth Without Violence.* New York: Knopf, 1975.

Madruga, Lenore. *One Step at a Time.* New York: McGraw-Hill, 1979.

Maslow, Abraham. *The Further Reaches of Human Nature.* New York: Viking, 1972.

Masterson, M.D. James F. *The Narcissistic and Borderline Disorders: An Integrated Developmental Approach.* New York: Brunner/Mazel, 1981.

McWilliams, Peter, and John-Roger. *You Can't Afford the Luxury of a Negative Thought.* Los Angeles: Prelude Press, 1988.

Milgram, Stanley. *Obedience to Authority.* New York: Harper Row, 1974.

Montagu, Ashley. *Life Before Birth.* New York: New American Library, Signet Books, 1965.

Rokeach, Milton. *The Nature of Human Values.* New York: Free Press, 1973.

Siegel, Daniel. *The Developing Mind: Toward a Neurobiology of Interpersonal Experience.* New York: Guilford Press, 1999.

Selye, Hans. *Stress Without Distress.* Philadelphia: J.B. Lippincott, 1974.

Sheehy, Gail. *Passages: Predictable Crises in Adult Life.* New York: E.P. Dutton, 1976.

Simonton, M.D. O. Carl, and Stephanie Matthews-Simonton, and James Creighton. *Getting Well Again.* Los Angeles: J.P. Tarcher, Inc., 1978.

Stern, D. *The First Relationship: Mother and Infant.* Cambridge, Mass., Harvard University Press, 1977.

Thomas, Alexander, and Stella Chess. *Temperment and Development.* New York: Brunner/Mazel, 1977.

Winnicott, D.W. *Playing and Reality.* London: Tavistock Publications Ltd., 1971.

Yalom, M.D. Irvin D. *The Gift of Therapy.* New York, HarperCollins, 2002.

Index

About the Author

Psychotherapist, counselor, supervisor, consultant and personal coach, Muriel James has authored or coauthored nineteen books including the 4.2 million-copy seller *Born to Win: Transactional Analysis and Gestalt Experiments*. Her books have been translated into 26 languages. She also has published seventeen journal articles and chapters in four books complied by others. Her recent book *Perspectives in Transactional Analysis* is a collection of her essays.

Muriel James holds two doctoral degrees and is an internationally known conference speaker. Her diverse audiences include the United Nations staff in Bangkok, the U. S. Navy Chaplains, the American Medical Association, and numerous universities, corporations, and professional and lay groups throughout the world.

Printed in the USA
CPSIA information can be obtained
at www.ICGtesting.com
JSHW012028140824
68134JS00033B/2933